"Our familiar paradigm of leadership is based on a male, military model of success, with winners and losers and, at the top, a hero figure who has reached the fifth and highest level of Maslow's hierarchy—self-actualization. But researchers who have explored outside this model of individual command and control have discovered a more effective style of leadership, one based on the capacity to use both analysis and empathy, and drawing on strengths traditionally associated with the interconnected, feeling world of women. This vision of leadership is not an either-or choice between "male" versus "female" styles, but an invitation to incorporate the many neglected aspects of cognitive, emotional, and behavioral empathy that transform transactional hierarchies into generative communities. In calling for a "Sixth Level" beyond self-actualization—"self-in-relation"—this book points to the need for all of us, no matter what position we hold, to move into an awareness of interconnectedness so that individuals, businesses, communities, and even the planet can thrive."

BETTY S. FLOWERS, PHD, former director of the LBJ Presidential Library and coauthor of *Presence: Human Purpose and the Field of the Future*

"This is the future of leadership! Incredibly researched and grounded in the real stories of successful women across industries, *The Sixth Level* offers a new leadership model for modern business. The authors create the ultimate guide for all leaders to use these critical strengths and groundbreaking management techniques to elevate their leadership. Take your career to the next level and unlock your potential with *The Sixth Level*."

DR. MARSHALL GOLDSMITH, Thinkers50 #1 Executive Coach and *New York Times* bestselling author of *The Earned Life, Triggers,* and *What Got You Here Won't Get You There*

"Leaders who use The Sixth Level model embrace human connection as fundamental to complex problem solving in organizations. Embedded in women's social psychology, ingenuity is one of the core differentiators the authors put forth to reach creative solutions that contribute to the trifecta: productive teams, sustainable communities, and profitability."

JOSH LINKNER, five-time tech entrepreneur, *New York Times* bestselling author, and venture capitalist

---

"At last—an intelligent and well-thought-out book on women's psychology that would benefit both male and female leaders alike. The authors draw from their personal inspirations and research to highlight unique and valuable aspects of women's leadership. Unlike many other books in this genre, this is not a rant, but a symphony of ideas that remind us why women are a vital part of the workforce, and how under-leveraged their personal capacities often are in a world previously defined by men. This is a must-read for anyone reflecting on leading in the 21st century."

SRINI PILLAY, M.D., Harvard-trained psychiatrist and brain researcher, faculty of Duke CE, McKinsey Think Tank Member, Chief Medical Officer and cofounder of Reulay, and CEO of NeuroBusiness Group

---

"It's not easy to be a female leader in a male-driven world, which is why this book is so incredibly necessary. *The Sixth Level* is next level because it teaches leaders everywhere that it is possible to build a successful business that is not only profitable, but also fosters connection and innovation, without the 24-7 hustle mentality."

MEL ROBBINS, bestselling author and host of the award-winning *Mel Robbins Podcast*

"This amazing book is full of heart and grounded in mindfulness. *The Sixth Level* is distinctive—it provides an honest critique of why we must move toward healthier relationships and more sustainable organizational culture. Along with new concepts and provocative questions, readers can consider for themselves how practicing the four core differentiators (mutuality, ingenuity, justness, and intrinsic motivation) will elevate their own leadership and the experience of their teams. The collection of narratives is compelling and shows us how to lead successfully at The Sixth Level."

CLAUDE SILVER, Chief Heart Officer, VaynerX, VaynerMedia

"What an epiphany! The male-dominated leadership model so popular in our culture is no longer sufficient, and we learn there is another, and better way. *The Sixth Level* reveals four differentiators, central to women's development, that enable higher level leadership. Their evidence-based sociology of leadership is underscored and amplified by case studies that demonstrate the multitude of competencies, strategies, insights, and principles that these women leaders deploy. This new and necessary narrative by women leaders teaches all of us, men and women, how to embrace and advance to The Sixth Level and drive organizational and community-wide excellence that brings necessary and sustainable change."

PATRICIA SPRATLEN ETEM, MPH, 1980 & 1984 Olympic Rower, founding member of the Independent Council on Women's Sports (ICONS) Rowing

"In the 1930s, my mother earned a bachelor's degree, then a master's, and founded Third Federal with my father. She didn't stop there. Her drive in a male-dominated industry shaped Third Federal and blazed the trail for those who came after her. Her values and compassion live on in how we conduct business to this day and highlight the importance of having women in leadership roles. Who knew that this was called Sixth Level Leadership!"

MARC A. STEFANSKI, chairman and CEO of Third Federal, and author of *People First: The Third Federal Way*

"To thrive in the future, leaders of organizations must take the initiative to operate at The Sixth Level to create intrinsically rewarding communities for work. The authors explain why The Sixth Level has been unrecognized throughout history and provide a guide for using this new model to build sustainable and profitable businesses. Read this book to learn the innovative practices from women leaders and entrepreneurs whose approaches were once overlooked but now are key."

RISHAD TOBACCOWALA, advisor, speaker, educator, and author of *Restoring the Soul of Business: Staying Human in the Age of Data*

"*The Sixth Level* is as profound as it is practical. In these pages, you will find an evolved model of leadership designed for a complex and unpredictable future. We've spent decades thinking and writing about leadership without the practice ever considering women's perspective on the subject. Sixth Level leadership recognizes the powerful psychological qualities developed in women, and incorporates them into four core differentiators that expand the leadership capabilities of leaders, both women and men. Gratitude sets the foundation and Sixth Level leadership moves us forward."

CHRIS SCHEMBRA, *Wall Street Journal* bestselling author of *Gratitude Through Hard Times* and *USA Today*'s "Gratitude Guru"

www.amplifypublishinggroup.com

*The Sixth Level: Capitalize on the Power of Women's Psychology
for Sustainable Leadership*

For more information, please contact:
Amplify Publishing, an imprint of Amplify Publishing Group
620 Herndon Parkway, Suite 220
Herndon, VA 20170
info@amplifypublishing.com

Library of Congress Control Number: 2023918383

CPSIA Code: PRV1123A

ISBN-13: 978-1-63755-856-0

Printed in the United States

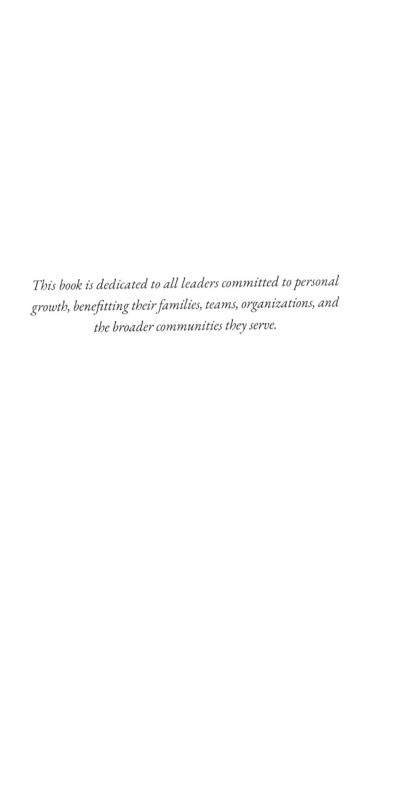

This book is dedicated to all leaders committed to personal growth, benefitting their families, teams, organizations, and the broader communities they serve.

JOIN THE MOVEMENT

THESIXTHLEVEL.COM

CAPITALIZE ON THE POWER OF WOMEN'S

PSYCHOLOGY FOR SUSTAINABLE

LEADERSHIP

THE SIXTH LEVEL

Stacy Feiner, PsyD   Kathy K. Overbeke, DBA

Jack D. Harris, PhD   Rachel Wallis Andreasson, MBA

CONTENTS

FOREWORD

By Ali Kindle Hogan, Founder and Chairperson, Rung for Women

"The most important thing in life is to be a good person."
—Jack Taylor, Founder of Enterprise Rent-A-Car, Ali's grandfather

GROWING UP IN MY family, leadership wasn't an option—it was a requirement. Because I was born into privilege and had the freedom to pour into activities and passions I was interested in, this wasn't taken lightly. From a very young age, I understood the importance of service to others, something I am very proud of, as it has guided me to where I am today.

I received the unique gift of being surrounded by a family of mostly women, a trait seventy-five years deep. I come from strong women, intelligent women, creative women—women who were and are still the backbone of my heritage. I saw substantial and tenacious ladies who were bold and effective in stewardship, and it is my hope to pass this along to my two girls. Seeing powerful female examples at such a young age instilled in me the foundation of helping others as part of my life's work—leadership from a woman's perspective is built into my DNA. And yet, one familial male did provide some influence as well.

When I was a child, my grandfather started a foundation. We grand-kids were required to take up a cause of our own to instill the value of philanthropy in us and to teach us the duty of paying it forward.

We literally had to pitch our ideas to him as if we were businesspeople in the boardroom. Imagine me at the tender age of ten, dressed in a professional blouse and slacks, trying to sell an idea to my grandfather and other family members. Beforehand, I needed to learn about organizations and promoting causes, as well as how to make appeals to "the board" so I could invest in my selected nonprofit.

Through this exercise, I learned the importance of being inquisitive and professional. I acquired knowledge about asking questions and preparing to receive feedback—good or bad. Back then, I had no idea this *Shark Tank* type of ritual would become the center and core of who I am and mold the organization I founded.

My grandfather and the women in my family not only shaped me into a future leader but prepped me to create a women's organization that instinctively understood female needs. My life today would not exist without first stepping into the family boardroom as a child after learning how to share my ideas, pitch them, and then lead the action steps.

Being a woman in leadership isn't an easy feat. You are often underestimated or pigeonholed into a category you probably won't fit into. Instead of others viewing you as a maverick or thought leader, some may see you as someone who checked off a box or who fit the required ratio. What they don't tell you, however, is that being a woman in a leadership position gives you a unique perspective that helps you guide others in a meaningful way.

A lot of men lead with power. Many women lead with emotion—too often perceived as a negative. But emotion cultivates vulnerability that enables us to self-correct and shift when necessary. Men tend to see things in black and white. Women see things more colorfully. We possess the benefit of allowing for shadows and changes in hues to emerge. With this advantage, we can become great leaders.

I have discovered a lot during my tenure as an organizational founder.

I've learned to accept failure and to invite feedback. I know recovering from something makes you grow. One of my biggest mistakes early on was not admitting that other people knew more than me—that others were smarter in some areas. A true leader understands that she doesn't have to be the most intelligent person in the room. But she does need the smarts to have the most intelligent person in the room sitting at her table.

Being a leader isn't singular—you need a qualified leadership team to teach and guide people with you. I am thankful to have a group of powerful women alongside me who are all great leaders. I've found women also feed off one another's strengths, which makes us more impactful.

With *The Sixth Level*, you have the opportunity to learn from women from all spectrums of leadership, careers, and experiences. Reading this book will help you tap into your self's highest capacity, therefore giving you the ability to soar to heights previously unknown. The Sixth Level leadership model provides a blueprint that will help you walk in your purpose effectively and with confidence.

Tapping into this final level is key. I look forward to utilizing this method myself as I continue Rung for Women's mission (www.rungforwomen.org) to inspire all women to climb the economic opportunity ladder. Please join me in this shift to an even deeper echelon of leadership development.

Alone, we can do many things. Together, we can achieve the highest level of personal and professional success.

Carrying the Torch

By Dr. Stacy Feiner

THE JOURNEY OF *The Sixth Level* began when, in high school, my mother introduced me to Dr. Jean Baker Miller and the Stone Center scholars at Wellesley College, where I learned that women's psychology develops differently than men's psychology and that women are complete human beings with undeniable qualities that foster potential in others. The powerful lectures and groundbreaking research ignited my career and passion to bring this psychology to business systems— to unleash the potential of leaders in ways that defy conventional narratives.

I bring this perspective to my work as a business psychologist to leaders of complex systems. Time and again, I collaborate with women and men leaders who are building inclusive cultures that people inherently want to join. Rachel Wallis Andreasson proved to be one of those leaders; she entered the scene in 2013 amid important leadership transitions in her family's business. She is a testament to the power of connection.

Through years of collaborating on projects and traveling into various settings with feminist ideals, we shared a leadership compass that brought us to 2021, when we asked, "What if?" What if we could crystallize decades of conversations and research, which have been sidelined, into a leadership movement? What if we showcased brilliant leadership rooted in the psychology of how women lead? What if we could eradicate the bias against women as emotional, risky, and complicated and instead prove these are the very qualities that allow women to lead better with a win-win-win formula? This framework we began to shape aimed at empowering people rather than controlling them.

I knew, based on years of coaching, that specific psychological qualities in women were elevating business performance and sustainability. I also observed that most male leaders gravitated toward this thinking once they saw how it worked. Conjuring business advisor Jim Collins, a student and teacher of what makes great companies, I also had collected a library of case studies and research-based insights from my own coaching. Themes about women's leadership surfaced and were proving successful in the business sector, but they were not broadly recognized or credited in the vast ocean of leadership books.

So Rachel and I started the work of writing a book. Rachel ignited the fire of collaboration. During this process, Rachel kept us laser focused on our shared goal while intuitively providing us the room for things to unfold.

We called on Kathy Overbeke to join the project because of her research expertise, entrepreneurial experience, and transformative powers. From entrepreneur to mother to academic, Kathy has conducted doctoral research that shines a light on the shadows of sexism that persist in family businesses. During this process, Kathy asked penetrating questions that got us to the heart of the matter.

Then after a series of conversations with Jack Harris, we were excited when he agreed to offer an expert male voice on the topic of gender relations to round us out. He was my beloved and inspirational college professor of sociology at Hobart and William Smith Colleges, where he inspired me to push the limits and reach my potential. For forty-nine years, he has guided students through the intricacies of sociology, and with colleagues established the first men's studies degree program in the US. During this process, Jack expanded our thinking while sharpening our findings, often referencing his exquisite work of rejuvenating state and local government agencies.

Together, Rachel, Kathy, Jack, and I converged our experiences and merged our passion projects, which set the stage for what ultimately became this book. *The Sixth Level* is a collaboration of four authors' life work and evidence of the magic that happens when a collective of committed individuals join forces. Each of us brings a unique perspective to weave into the model you'll read about here.

The contributors, an astounding group of women leaders, have provided real, raw, and authentic stories to illustrate our thesis. They show how they used unconventional leadership qualities at pivotal moments in their companies that improved employees' experiences and yielded greater results. They took a leap of faith, engaged fully and authentically. They realized there are many women leaders, like them, who have embraced *The Sixth Level*. *The Sixth Level* elevates leadership and offers a new paradigm.

This book is a manifestation of our shared vision of leadership for the future. Please read these pages with an open heart and embark on a journey that explores the remarkable influence social psychology has on elevating leadership. You will discover the power of shared vision and the allure of collaboration. And you'll see how thinking differently about leadership—focusing on our best human qualities—can transform individuals, teams, families, and communities. As Rachel always says, people come into your life for a reason. Thank you for inviting us into yours.

INTRODUCTION

How to Use This Book

What to Expect

The book is a jumping-off point. The Sixth Level is a bold new leadership framework that challenges conventional assumptions about leadership. We invite you to carefully consider the leadership and relational gaps that may exist in you, your leadership team, and your organization whether you are looking from the top down or the bottom up. This new framework is a litmus test for a new standard of leadership that will better serve organizations and humanity.

The time is right. There is an energy for change, and there is a groundswell fueled by four intense global systemic disruptors: the health pandemic, ethnic and racial unrest, global economic distress, and an environmental crisis. The data is clear: we are in an incredibly unstable, unsustainable state. Our lives are emotionally, socially, and relationally strained, which skews the ways in which we engage the world and ourselves. People are ready to seize a new level of leadership.

The Sixth Level points the way. This book is educational and practical. On the educational side, you will learn the impact of leadership models that are defined and dominated by a patriarchal system. You will see the invisible rules that define, direct, and cloud the way we live and lead, and you will begin to recognize how self-actualization, the fifth level of Maslow's hierarchy of needs, is not enough. We will introduce a new level of actualization: Self-in-Relation, which is based on human connections. We will immerse you in the research and theories that support this framework in Chapter 3 and throughout the book.

On the practical side, we discover through the narratives of seasoned leaders that their experiences and leadership approaches achieved significant results utilizing four Core Differentiators: Mutuality, Ingenuity, Justness, and Intrinsic Motivation, which set the foundation of The Sixth Level.

What This Book Is

This is a leadership book that describes a mindset and accompanying behaviors that transform the conventional paradigms of leadership.

It challenges us to find our authenticity in relation to others. It rejects formulaic scripts and roles; it embraces a "feeling intellect" (Rieff 1975). It connects and appreciates others, dispels fear and alienation, and fosters a sense of belonging and partnership.

The four Core Differentiators, when practiced together, elevate individuals, teams, and organizations through unifying principles that serve human interests. We explain the definitions of these in Chapter 1 and share examples of them in Chapters 5 through 8.

What You Will Discover

- A critique of the patriarchal paradigm that has systematically rendered invisible and rejected critical forms of women's leadership that contribute to more just communities.

- Strategies and techniques for the workplace that embrace Dr. Jean Baker Miller and the Stone Center scholars' theory on women's social psychology.
- Models of Sixth Level leadership through exemplary cases by women leaders.

Based on women's social psychology, *The Sixth Level* argues that women have more often and characteristically demonstrated forms of leadership based on human connection, which are Self-in-Relation. The characteristics of such leadership stand in contrast to leadership based on forms of domination and control. You will see these differences as you read each contributor's narrative in Chapters 5 through 8.

Our contributors lead organizations that collectively represent over $18.7 billion in annual revenue and over 47,000 employees. Each narrative recounts a specific point in time when the leader faced a challenge or opportunity that impacted their entire organization. Each leader reveals her principles and practices that enabled her to tackle the challenge or leverage the opportunity using unconventional and sometimes less tested strategies. These narratives illustrate a leadership approach to sustainable and profitable operations and change. Embedded in these illustrations are leadership principles that have improved the performance of the company organizationally and/or financially. In many of the cases, the exemplars express what they wanted the people in their workforce to experience.

The chapters also describe successful outcomes and how they served the entire organization. For example, what worked for Andreasson's situation wouldn't have necessarily worked in Slesh's, but lessons from each can be applied to any workplace.

What This Book Is Not

This is not a "women's book."

This is a book for all of us who want to bring vitality to our organizations that is generative and affirming. Such leadership rejects hierarchies of power that are primarily transactional rather than relational.

This is not a "blame game."

There is a difference in identifying and critiquing systems versus blaming people. In this regard, we contrast conventional leadership, which is entrenched in the patriarchal social system, to Sixth Level leadership. Both men and women are harmed by the worst of patriarchy and have been subject to its socializations. We did not make the system, but we are in it, we sustain it, and we have a hard time breaking through barriers because we are immersed in it. We have adapted to its demands or risked suffering stigmatization. But we are conscious and self-conscious beings, fully able, once we see it, to move toward our own health and the health of others. If you see that harm has resulted from your leadership practice, there is an alternative. The contributors' narratives provide all of us with an awareness that there are different and better, healthier, and more sustainable ways to lead.

While we can each do our own individual part, together we can move more quickly and create an effective movement toward a new paradigm. *The Sixth Level* makes us ask tough questions of ourselves, our leaders, and the people in our organizations.

This does not solve all the world's problems.

When we stop and consider all the world's problems, from politics to the environment, for example, we can easily be overwhelmed. As such, the book limits its subjects to leadership and business. However, this book is a gateway, and when applied, the principles and processes can inform and facilitate the success of every healing cause and movement. We know that collectively we can do more than individually.

This is not a wait-and-see book.

This is a book that will make you think about the paradigms within which you live and how you might be contributing to our paralysis. We challenge readers to reflect on collective human history and think about our current state. Understand The Sixth Level and how each of the core differentiators work so that together we can create a movement, an ingenious way to move forward.

What Are the Takeaways of Each Section?

This book is set up to educate, offer viable and practical solutions, and prompt action through reflective exercises and activities.

Section One: Capitalize on the Power of Women's Psychology for Sustainable Leadership provides the reader with an understanding that the cause of our crisis is systemic. Looking from the outside in, this book calls out a system that has infiltrated our thinking and our ways of living and has clouded our vision on what it takes to be a caring leader.

To achieve our collective goals for creating sustainable communities that reach better financial returns, the reader should understand the psychological concept of toggling and how this activates the four Core Differentiators that lead to Sixth Level leadership.

Section Two: Case Studies of Sixth Level Leadership provides powerful personal narratives from seasoned leaders who demonstrate how Sixth Level leadership has achieved better outcomes for their organizations and their people. With a synthesis of lessons learned about the Core Differentiators, readers will have models and tactics to practice themselves in their own organizations.

Section Three: The Sixth Level Advantage summarizes the model that produces better outcomes. The afterword shares a vision of what is possible when The Sixth Level is understood, adopted, and implemented. You will achieve compounded value using the reflective exercises that can help you be a more effective leader, create more unified teams, and build more sustainable organizations.

Call to Action

Each one of us has amazing power to influence and engage those around us. *The Sixth Level* demonstrates that a Self-in-Relation mindset combined with strong mutuality yields sustainable change and gains momentum for a movement.

PAUSE.
Think about what is at stake.
Feel the energy for change.

NOTICE.
How the system distorts our humanity.
How much further our shared humanity could take us.

ACT.
Be better. Do better. Together.
NOW!

This is a call to action.

Capitalize on the Power of Women's Psychology for Sustainable Leadership

CHAPTER 1

Self-in-Relation Theory: A Leadership Revolution

"Disconnection is the source of human suffering."
—Dr. Jean Baker Miller, Women in Connection

What the Hell Is Water?

There are two young fish swimming along who happen to meet an older fish. The older fish nods at them and says, "Morning, boys. How's the water?" The two young fish swim on for a bit, and then eventually one of them looks over at the other and asks, "What the hell is water?"

David Foster Wallace's (2005) famous commencement fish story at Kenyon College illustrates how easy it is to fail to see what's right in front of us. We unconsciously adhere to societal norms and are blind to roles we inhabit that harm others, our relationships, and ourselves.

In the pages that follow, we explain and illustrate how applying Self-in-Relation theory provides a model for leadership that is more effective, more profitable, more sustainable, and fundamentally much more successful—a model that shows leaders why conventional leadership comes up short, and how building intrinsically rewarding communities yields even greater profitability.

FIGURE 1. THE SIXTH LEVEL

The Sixth Level™

The strength of this new model is its capacity to give every community the chance to reach healthy and fair social dynamics. *The Sixth Level* recognizes the universal value of women's proclivity for mutuality and the practice of care to take us beyond leadership defined by dominance—a framework that gives all versions of community, families, businesses, governments, institutions, and human service organizations the ability to reorganize around well-being and emotional health.

Abraham Maslow (1954) asserted a hierarchy of five needs that ended at self-actualization, the highest measure of human development and the pinnacle of psychological well-being. Maslow believed that once individuals have first met their lower-level needs, they can focus on pursuing personal growth, achieving one's unique potential, and fulfilling personal goals and aspirations. Like many contemporary theorists of that time whose research was based almost exclusively on men, Maslow prematurely concluded that psychological development peaked at self-actualization, represented as separation and autonomy.

We call on all leaders to strive beyond Maslow's fifth level of self-actualization—to The Sixth Level (see Figure 1: The Sixth Level), which we call Self-in-Relation, named for the theory based on Dr. Jean Baker Miller's work on women's psychology. In 1976, Miller wrote *Toward A New Psychology of Women* to dispute a significant flaw in prior psychological research. Until this time, almost all psychological research was conducted on male subjects and the findings were erroneously generalized to women (Gilligan 1982; Sterling 1992). Women were therefore consistently found to be deviant from the male norm (Robb 2006).

Miller's insight that " . . . women's sense of self becomes very organized around being able to make and then maintain affiliations and relationships" (1976, 83) points to the critical importance of emotional connection, reciprocity of care, and mutuality of self and other (see Figure 2: The Dynamic of Self-in-Relation). Ignoring this model could simply leaves us in a system that is dysfunctional and limits our ability to be great leaders.

There is a groundswell of voices in all aspects of society, including business, expressing the need for a better social structure. The volume of voices, their expansiveness, and the intense dissatisfaction signify that we are at a point where the pain of staying the same is greater than the pain of making deliberate change. We are motivated.

FIGURE 2. THE DYNAMIC OF SELF-IN-RELATION

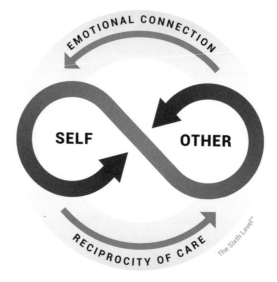

This business book intends to challenge your mindset, your leadership teams, and your organization to embrace a new model where you and others work and grow in connection. When practiced collectively, this new leadership model will make change possible—sustainable and profitable—to advance us all.

Just as all the contributors to this book—business owners, executives, CEOs, and entrepreneurs—have chosen to lead with new principles, you as a reader must decide whether to keep spinning your wheels in the current system and its processes and policies or to band with other leaders working to elevate us to a new paradigm.

Reality Is Skewed

People used to think the earth was flat. When it was discovered that the earth is round, everyone's belief system had to change. Psychologically, it meant we were relieved of the anxiety about accidentally falling off the side of the earth. Scientifically, it meant new fields of research and human potential could be explored.

While all industries have evolved dramatically over the centuries, our framework for how society is structured—and how leadership should be practiced—has not gone far enough, especially in its recognition of women's leadership contributions.

This unexamined framework is built on a patriarchal system of leadership, the biases it creates, and perpetuations that often render women invisible. It is a framework that has disenfranchised women— and deprived all of us of the essential strengths that women bring to the table. It is nonsense to assert that women are the weaker sex, ignoring the fact that women endure childbirth and have typically been responsible for the well-being of their families and their communities.

The framework is a remnant of our mythological past in which men were seen as strong and natural leaders and women were seen as weak and domesticated. This remains the system that pervades organizations, companies, governments, and culture. It is not the "preferred" system; it *is* the system, the water in which we swim. It is a hierarchical, command-and-control model that often results in exclusion, disenfranchisement, frustration, alienation, and despair in men and women. The consequence to men for leaving patriarchy unchallenged is the requirement that they denounce their own needs for emotional connection.

In short, we live in a world where wielding power is the defining characteristic of leadership.

Unsustainable Paradigm

Yet this persistent framework is not the natural order of things. It is an artificial construct that has gained unprecedented power as each generation blindly accepts this false narrative and inevitably creates lies that reinforce it. As an example, American psychologist Dr. Lawrence Kohlberg (1958) essentially labeled women as morally inferior to men, basing his claim on deeply flawed research done exclusively on male subjects and asserting that men demonstrated higher-order abstract moral thinking. He implied that women lacked moral reasoning skills. Dr. Carol Gilligan (1982), Harvard professor of psychology, disputes Kohlberg's findings—in her book, *In a Different Voice*, she demonstrates using her own research that women's moral reasoning is different. It is relational, based on compassion and an "ethic of care." Yet the scientific community has left Kohlberg's findings intact and has not required him to retract his assertion.

Yes, there have been women leaders: prime ministers, queens, and pharaohs. But the traits that we have associated with "good leaders" are almost exclusively male. Autonomy. Power. Authority. Competition. Conquest. Toughness. Lack of emotion. All leaders, both female and male, have been judged by these metrics, and those who have excelled in them have been lauded, rewarded, and promoted.

Meanwhile, the water in which we swim is dangerously polluted. Essential and distinctly "female" qualities have been ignored, devalued, and pathologized. Leaders, whether female or male, who prioritize these "softer" characteristics, such as acts of empathy, caretaking, and emotional expression, do so at their own risk, being viewed as "softer," "feminine," and "motherly" and being discredited and forsaken. Through the lens of patriarchy, the nurturing emotions expected of women equate to losing whereas aggressive emotions such as anger, dominance, and detachment expected of men equate to winning. Caring is seen as subservient. Collaborating is seen as giving away power. When women operate in these ways, especially in business or leadership roles, they have been accused of being needy

. . . immature . . . weak . . . naive . . . unreliable . . . motherly. More lies that skew our reality.

Patriarchy's definition of leadership, one built on power, control, and a winner-take-all mentality, is harmful to society and catastrophic for women. The tragic consequences are best captured in Shel Silverstein's *The Giving Tree* (1964). The beautiful and strong mother tree provides shade, comfort, respite, and delight to the boy. He plays on her branches, he carves his initials in her trunk, and he eats her apples. But as the boy grows, he keeps taking from her, and she keeps giving. First, he harvests all her apples to sell. Then he uses her branches for lumber to build a home. Then he cuts down her trunk to make a boat. No matter what he takes, the Giving Tree keeps giving everything she can, everything she has left to offer, until the end, when the majestic mother tree has been reduced to a stump on which the old man rests, blind to what has been destroyed.

Is this a lesson about giving or stealing? The tale celebrates that women constitute themselves by being selfless. The selfless tree doesn't complain; she has been told to accommodate, even at the price of her own demise. If the boy and the tree had learned to communicate their respective needs and agreed to a reciprocal partnership, both emotional and practical, they could have built a mutually beneficial relationship. Applied to business, the story is even more revealing. Must we destroy what nurtures us, rejecting care and mutual reward and concern for others to achieve success? Must one person's success come at another's destruction?

There is mounting evidence that when organizations embrace inclusion, mutual respect, justness, and the ethic of care (Gilligan 1982), they reap *even greater* success, growth, profits, and sustainability . . . and for more people.

In business, we have been told that drive, profits, competition, earnings, ambition, and success are incompatible with empathy, collaboration, inclusion, nurture, and justness. When leaders believe they must choose between profits and growth on the one hand and inclusion and justness on the other hand, they feel obligated to choose profits—and they reject an ethic of care. It is the defining characteristic of patriarchal leadership. And when the definition of success excludes consideration of well-being, motivation, and sustainability, leaders excuse themselves from civic responsibilities of justness, mutuality, and intrinsic motivation. Under patriarchy, even "enlightened leaders" can claim they cannot afford to sacrifice the bottom line to accommodate the "soft" benefits.

Social Psychological Reset

People are calling for better forms of leadership, as we discuss in Chapter 3, but the paradigm within which leadership currently operates, while accepting technological and medical change, for example, resists gender equity. Sixth Level leadership requires a thoughtful examination of how patriarchy has framed our psychology and business practices. While Jean Baker Miller disrupted beliefs about women's psychology and healthy psychology for all people, beliefs set out by Kohlberg, Maslow and other men still dominate our culture. These dominate beliefs perpetuate claims that women are inferior and thus justify their being marginalized from business and leadership. Therefore, and also not surprisingly, the definition of a good leader—and all the rewards associated—have been based on perfecting self-actualization. Ironically, in practice, "self-actualization" devolves into selfishness.[1]

In 1972, Jean Baker Miller and the Stone Center scholars at Wellesley College conducted research that offered a new way of organizing families, communities, culture, and society. Miller presents compelling evidence of a different motivation for human behavior based on *relationships* as a central human need. Miller argues that we learn about ourselves through our interactions with others and our emotional connections with others. She makes a compelling argument that women bear a psychology that elevates their humanity and leadership to its highest potential. By extension, great leaders regardless of gender, must reach this level too, so they are able to think and act beyond their own self-interest and self-direction. In this book, we demonstrate that The Sixth Level processes rely on mutuality, which is the foundation for the development of an authentic self.

Today we know how right she was. And with this book, we know how to implement her theories and change the future. We start by valuing essential and distinctly "female" qualities such as empathy, caretaking, and expressions of emotion. We stop denigrating the traits of "soft," "feminine," and "motherly." We stop celebrating aggressive emotions such as anger, dominance, and detachment. We start embracing collaboration and care. Degree by degree, we can and will shift the corporate American paradigm.

A New Leadership Paradigm: Self-in-Relation

As a society, we have devalued and discouraged women's contributions to leadership throughout the centuries (Boulding 1976). In the worst cases, women have been silenced and bullied for trying to contribute and speak up. Even at the Stone Center, a small but mighty pocket of women scholars were dismissed by mainstream psychology and left out of the scientific journals. Compelled by their own findings, they pushed on and contributed to significant work in women's psychology and the contemporary practice of psychotherapy.

Even when organizations and individuals attempt to use the valuable capabilities that are unique to women in a command-and-control culture, they fall short. And when this happens, it appears that leaders are simply giving lip service to inclusion and well-being. These inclusive qualities end up as window dressing for the command-and-control leadership paradigm. They become empty promises from empty suits. Look, for example, at Kouzes and Posner, *The Leadership Challenge: How to Make Extraordinary Things Happen in Organizations* (2023), now in its 7th Edition. The book's five practices are considered the bible for leadership. But where are the women? Where is any recognition of the gender discrepancies in who gets to lead?

But just imagine, for a moment, a better way: a model of leadership based on women's social psychology, where protection is achieved through an ethic of care, in which nurturing others is the way for all to prosper. It is a model that evolves from top-down buy-in to intrinsic motivation, from one-sided empathy to two-way mutuality, and from command and control to ingenuity and justness. In this model, growth and profits improve, as do the health and vitality of the entire organization (Simon Sinek 2017).

As you will see in the case studies in this book, this new model of leadership is already sprouting up in companies and organizations throughout the world. These cases expose the false dichotomy in which reason is pitted against emotion. Sixth Level leadership, toggling between empathy and analysis (see Chapter 3), creates opportunity, meaning, empowerment, voice, and success for all. It is generative with a bias toward abundance and collective reward.

This model benefits all leaders, and all genders, as we shall see in Chapter 2.

Our contributors offer a groundbreaking and eye-opening collection of practices of women leaders operating at The Sixth Level. Right before our eyes, we have research and data that disrupts the status quo. They tell a very different story from the past and point the way to a new model of leadership. This model is unique because it unearths and confirms Self-in-Relation theory as a powerful explanation of human development; it draws on the work of several brilliant social scientists who expand on Miller's work, further exploring and showing that women's focus on relationships suggests a more evolved model for organizational development and interpersonal relations. It offers four Core Differentiators that, when individually and collectively applied, elevate us into a new, sustainable paradigm. And finally, it applies this understanding of women's social psychology to leadership.

The Four Core Differentiators of Sixth Level Leadership

Based on the work of Jean Baker Miller and the Stone Center scholars, Dr. Stacy Feiner (2018) hypothesized four Core Differentiators that support a new model of leadership subsequently called in this book The Sixth Level. Let us look at each of these differentiators and examine what they mean for future leaders and the specific qualities the leader exemplifies to create, with the team, a sustainable culture.

Mutuality

Mutuality is the ability to engender an emotional connection between two people where there is a genuine exchange of "experiencing each other" and "influencing each other"—think of it as mutual empathy where concern flows both ways.

Ingenuity

Ingenuity is the ability to invent novel solutions that serve the interests of many. This ability requires the leader to toggle between empathic and analytic understanding.

Justness

Justness is the mechanism for organizations and communities to operate optimally together, requiring fair and full representation, transparent and consistent procedures for ensuring due process, the fostering of a sense of belonging and cohesion, and ultimately the freedom to pursue purpose.

Intrinsic Motivation

Intrinsic motivation is the emotional drive to go above and beyond one's narrow self-interest for mutually rewarding and beneficial outcomes within a community or organization where the community is mutually invested in shared outcomes.

When a leader models these four Core Differentiators and the leader and their team hold each other accountable for these qualities, it advances the entire team. The qualities shown by women leaders—mutuality, ingenuity, justness, and the intrinsic motivation that follows—provide a sure path for healthier, more successful organizations across the board. These qualities aren't limited to women, nor are they only available to female leaders. Men can take the lessons from these success stories and apply these same four concepts to business, to society, and to culture. They can be part of the paradigm shift and not just change the workforce but be an integral part of shaping a better, more empathetic next generation. Imagine how that would change the water and shift the currents for the entire world.

The four core differentiators, when practiced together, lessen the risk for the misuse of power. When put into practice, this framework allows leaders to create the conditions necessary for intrinsically-rewarding cultures. We don't have to search for a way—the qualities needed for sustainable and prosperous communities have always been there, evolving within women for all leaders to learn. Take a moment to imagine how applying the core differentiators, collectively as leaders, could generate the momentum to shift the current for all boats to rise.

A New World

Some companies have been trying out new leadership models based on mutuality and relationships, and we need more of them. But what happens when they don't see the water they are swimming in? What happens when they remain sold on the myth that inclusion and care come at the cost of profits and growth? When times are flush, they don't feel the pressure. But as soon as times get tough, they walk away from the people side and retreat to command and control.

Contrast this with the story of Lisa Lochner, the first female CEO of Sullivan Hospital. Sullivan is the only hospital in a large radius, and it serves a lot of people, including many underprivileged people. Lisa's motto when she became CEO was "One Heart, One Team." She struggled to take the position because she felt uncomfortable taking something that so many colleagues also wanted. Stacy told her, "They don't know this the way you do. When you become the CEO, you're going to take all of the things you wanted to do and change when you were one of them, and you're going to make those things happen. You're going to help them do their jobs better. They don't need to be the CEO; they just need the *right* CEO." When leaders have a personal relationship with the business, they're compelled to make things right. That's what Lisa did at Sullivan Hospital.

The Sixth Level as a model for leadership is just as revolutionary and just as clearly true. It is also *necessary*. When women are silenced, they are ineffective or unable to deliver, and neither men nor women enjoy the benefits. The female qualities shown by the women leaders in this book—mutuality, ingenuity, justness, and intrinsic motivation that follows—provide a path for healthier and more successful organizations across the board. Women have these qualities, and they are responsible for delivering them—to individuals, to their teams, and to their communities.

The Sixth Level model of leadership is a commitment to all leaders and all organizations. While the book foregrounds women leaders and a form of leadership more historically reflective of women leaders, this is a book for everyone. The Sixth Level model is a way to help all of us bravely face the future—wiser, safer, and happier. It is life-affirming.

CHAPTER 2

Engendering Leadership: Beyond Patriarchy

"Every man must decide whether he will walk in the light of creative altruism or in the darkness of destructive selfishness. This is the judgment. Life's most urgent question is: What are you doing for others?"
—Martin Luther King Jr.

ONCE MALE PRIVILEGE AND sexism vividly come to light, once it is made plain to you, especially by someone who you hold in high regard, you can never say you didn't know. Here is Jack's story:

It was the late 1970s, and my spouse Deb and I had agreed to an arrangement about cooking and dishwashing—when one of us cooked, the other one cleaned. I thought myself a nascent feminist, but the arrangement soured when the dishes I was scheduled to clean built up, festering in the sink. Deb challenged my resistance to fulfill my part of the bargain. Reading the framed saying over our sink gifted to her by her dad, "Don't hurry, don't worry, and don't forget to smell the flowers," I made the mistaken inference and told Deb, "You like doing the dishes; I hate doing the dishes," to which she replied, with considerable animation, that she too hated doing the dishes, that it was a [expletive] job. That was the first of the "bricks to my head" that starkly revealed my own unawareness of my assumptions about the worlds of women and men. I was, in fact, a sexist. To be exposed by a person who I loved, with whom I was building a relationship, made it even more hurtful. Sexism was not only "out there;" I had brought it home.

Tragically (and it does result in tragedies) sexism is a persistent cultural pattern that organizes and distributes power and rewards based on sex difference. For example, in the United States, income differences are apparent based on gender for the same work. Most recently, we have seen that COVID-19 affected women in their workplaces, and they had to leave their jobs or cut back on hours because of the absence of day care. Men were not similarly affected, as they more often than not are not responsible for childcare (McKinsey & Company 2021).[1]

Our socialization to a patriarchal ideology that includes male domination, sexism and the subordination of women, the almost exclusive use of violence by men, and heterosexism and discrimination against LGBTQ+ people has distorted our images of women and men. This distortion of women usually means that women are excluded, under-promoted, or not heard, and they are kept out of leadership positions because they are read as too emotional and weak. This creates self-doubt about their abilities. This distortion of men involves scripts that demand toughness with a narrow selection of emotions and an underlying anxiety about proving their masculinity.

These distortions have created a problematic discourse between the sexes that has, in effect, defined women as inferior to a male norm both when they act like women and when they act like men (Schur 1984), a classic double bind. It defends gender arrangements through innumerable rationalizations and denials and sustains a system of gender norms that act as a mechanism for the social control of women and men. This unequal status has been supported by the reality that in patriarchal society, "being female carries a stigma in and of itself" (Laws 1979). However, it is important to realize that these ideological claims are less about actual sex differences but rather about how power and place are distributed. While many men do not express the worst traits of patriarchy, men as a group still benefit from its privileges vis-à-vis women.

Thus the differential but intertwined life worlds of men and women are sociological entities: they are the cultural structures of laws, customs, mores, traditions, attitudes, and beliefs into which both female and male infants, respectively, are born and are differentially shaped, shaped to contribute to their gendered part of the pattern, and shaped to find the patterns tolerable.

Femininity and masculinity are constructions of a form of "gender tyranny" in which everyone is trapped and in which individuals who do not conform to the traditional gender binary are marginalized and even erased from public discourse. As subjects to patriarchy's arbitrary power that is supported by the fear of going against its tacitly enveloped ideology, everyone is locked into gendered roles, and these roles have very narrow bandwidth. This ideology of hegemonic masculinity (Connell 1995),[2] its denial of the feminine and unpatriarchal, and its deviance from the traditional gender binary become supported through a ubiquitous propaganda that "serves to emancipate thought from experience and reality . . ." (Arendt 1951, 471).

Sexism and Disconnection

Sexism is so ordinary, so matter-of-fact, that unless forced to see it, most men and many women simply do not have it in their frame of reference. Double standards are the evidence of sexism, but until we are asked to see it, most accept gender inequality as the natural order of things. But this could not be less true.

Society is contrived to serve those in power. Our entire reality is based on doctrines of men's psychology in almost every field. Daily, we enact divisions of labor, forms of leadership, and forms of relationships that are taken for granted and routinely enforce gender roles and gender stereotypes. We live and work in a gendered system, which we believe has worked. But it is deeply dysfunctional. In almost all cases, these systems subordinate women and privilege men. McKinsey & Company's report on "Women in the Workplace 2022" amply documents this:

"Women leaders are switching jobs at the highest rates we've ever seen—and at higher rates than men in leadership. This could have serious implications for companies. Women are already significantly underrepresented in leadership. For years, fewer women than men have risen through the ranks because of the "broken rung" at the first step up to management. Now companies are struggling to hold on to the relatively few women leaders they have. And all these dynamics are even more pronounced for women of color.

The reasons women leaders are stepping away from their companies are telling. Women leaders are just as ambitious as men, but at many companies, they face headwinds that signal it will be harder to advance. They are more likely to experience belittling microaggressions, such as having their judgment questioned or being mistaken for someone more junior. They are doing more to support employee well-being and foster inclusion, but this critical work is spreading them thin and goes mostly unrewarded. And finally, it's increasingly important to women leaders that they work for companies that prioritize flexibility, employee well-being, and diversity, equity, and inclusion.

If companies do not act, they risk losing not only their current women leaders but also the next generation of women leaders. Young women are even more ambitious and place a higher premium on working in an equitable, supportive, and inclusive workplace. They are watching senior women leave for better opportunities, and they're prepared to do the same" (McKinsey & Company 2022, Introduction).

Patriarchal systems have been so encompassing that men have not recognized the destruction that is inflicted on women and other men, including what is self-inflicted. Men have created what Andrew Kimbrell has named, in parallel to Betty Friedan, the author of *The Feminine Mystique* (1963), the "masculine mystique" (Kimbrell 1995), in which the image of men is one that is autonomous, efficient, intensely self-interested, and disconnected from community and the earth. Psychoanalyst Dr. Nancy Chodorow tells us that to establish male gender identity, the male child must disconnect from the mother and connect as best as possible with a mostly absent and often distant father (Chodorow 1999), while the female child develops her identity firmly in the light and embrace of her mother. For male development, this has resulted in a psychology of disconnection and dismissal of strong emotional bonds. Therefore, what are magnified and valued as the healthy psychological norms are autonomy, separation, and individuation (Piaget 1932; Kohlberg 1958). As early as four years old, boys are already performing masculinity, disconnecting from their emotions (Chu 2014). In her study of boys, Niobe Way concludes that boys have a crisis of connection. Says Way:

> Just as our masculine stereotypes rest on constructs of autonomy and stoicism, so does our definition of maturity—revealing, of course, the patriarchy at work, with manhood meaning the same thing as adulthood . . . Rather than privileging the self-sufficient and autonomous elements, boys (and girls) suggest that we should emphasize the relational components of maturity—especially given our current crisis of connection . . . Being self-sufficient

and independent are, of course, valuable parts of being mature, but we are hurting ourselves, as the boys suggest, when we focus almost exclusively on those elements of maturity . . . we should see boys' and girls' social and emotional skills and their ability to have mutually supportive relationships as a significant part of the meaning of maturity itself. (Way 2013, 232)

Indeed, the masculine mystique teaches men that successful businessmen must be strong and competitive, and men must avoid emotions that might lead to caring and loving (business is war; it is not personal). It celebrates the ethics of independence and distancing—it turns men against women and against one another (see Figure 3: The Social Psychological Gender Gap). As we show later in this chapter, systems built on male supremacy are deeply harmful, wounding both women and men, actually limiting our organizational and business success, and at great cost to us as human beings. There is a better way.

FIGURE 3. THE SOCIAL PSYCHOLOGICAL GENDER GAP

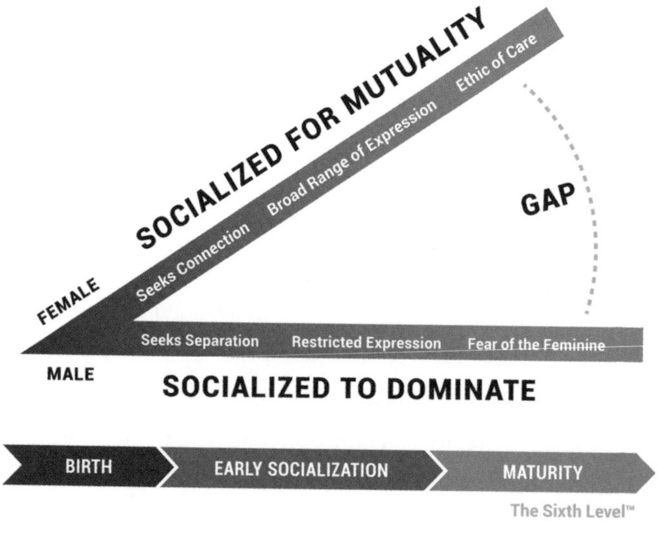

The Mindset of Connection

Jean Baker Miller, in *Toward a Psychology of Women*, helps us see that women have more often and characteristically demonstrated forms of leadership based on **human connection** understood as Self-in-Relation. The characteristics of leadership based on Self-in-Relation stand in contrast to leadership based on forms of domination and patriarchy. Jordan, Walker, and Hartling (2004, 13-14) further help us to distinguish the myths of the "male model" of leadership as distinct from its opposite, Self-in-Relation.

The dominant myths of instrumental competence, which largely coincide with the myths of masculinity, include:

1. The myth that competition enhances performance.
2. The myth of invulnerability.
3. The myth of certainty, what I call the cultivation of pathological certainty.
4. The myth of self-sufficiency ("I did it alone; so can you").
5. The myth of mastery ("I mastered it; I am the master").
6. The myth of objectivity.
7. The myth of the expert.
8. The myth of unilateral change (in an interaction, the less powerful person is changed).
9. The myth of hierarchy, that ranking produces incentives, and that people assume their places in the hierarchy by virtue of merit.
10. The myth that power over others creates safety.
11. The myth that rational engagement is superior to and at odds with emotional responsiveness.

More profoundly, Jean Baker Miller recognizes the behavior that characterizes the social psychology of Self-in-Relation is grounded in women's experience of and in patriarchies.[3] Her point is not that women are born this way naturally; on the contrary, Miller has a keen sense of context. The first is that women have demonstrated a leadership rendered invisible, unrecognized, and dismissed as leadership. *Why?* Because women have served primarily in the domestic sphere since they were excluded, made diminutive, and made subservient in the public sphere. The second is that this leadership, exemplified by women and demonstrated by our cases in Chapters 5 through 8, has certain properties, which we describe as The Sixth Level, that are differentiated by mutuality, ingenuity, justness, and intrinsic motivation and are arguably more effective, sustainable, and profitable.

This foundation for the subordination of women by men is brilliantly explained by Elise Boulding in her virtually invisible 1976 book, *The Underside of History: A View of Women through Time*, which comprehensively and meticulously documents the invisibility of women's lives, their leadership, and their critical contributions to humanity throughout human history. Boulding reveals that with rare exceptions, women have lived in the underside of societies and their histories. Women activities are oriented predominantly around human welfare in all social classes, and men's activities are oriented predominantly around conquest and dominance (Boulding 1976, 8). These differences are part of a persistent social-historical pattern that results in a difference in the psychology of the sexes—behind every psychology is a sociology. While Boulding recognizes biological attributes, she concludes that the social invisibility of women is a cultural and conceptual artifact. For millennia the role of women in the household and in their communities has been underestimated and undervalued. "This has made understandings and policies about sex-based roles particularly resistant to those processes of social change that reshape other social roles" (Boulding 1976, 9).

This is quite a remarkable conclusion after an examination of gender in the sweep of Western history—that social power, especially today, is not legitimately based on the claimed differences in biological attributes[4] but rather on a cultural and historical artifact that has persisted because of patriarchal socialization and its enforcements. Indeed:

> Dominance systems organize most of our political and economic life. Furthermore, since they are also primarily male dominance systems, they cast an extra shadow over the life of women, both in the public and domestic spheres. Men and women alike, but men more than women, are used to being rewarded for doing what society values by being given a "dominance" bank account. (Boulding 1976, 47–48)

Most people cannot imagine that sex roles are as flexible as they are. We don't see it as a sociological contrivance. Not only are sex and gender *roles* socially prescribed, but gender in and of itself is a social construction that systematically excludes, marginalizes, and endangers those who do not fall into or subscribe to the binary.

Leadership has been mainly understood as a male trait and women leaders as an anomaly. As a result, the experiences of women are ignored and misunderstood, their voices silenced, and their contributions undervalued. Such an example appeared in the *New York Times* on April 26, 2023. Jennifer Grose reports that fathers are not embracing domestic work, as it is not valued (Grose 2023). Indeed, it is old news— Hochschild (2003) has amply identified the "second shift" where women work outside the home but still are expected to handle the domestic responsibilities before and after work. Other evidence: in a study looking at the data from 1950 to 2000, there is clear evidence that pay declines when an occupation becomes female-dominated in what was a male-dominated occupation (Levanon, England, and Allison 2009).

Finally, Boulding points to the important and unacknowledged role of the household and the origins of women's leadership, a social psychology, and its behavior that Miller called "Self-in-Relation" and what this book embraces as The Sixth Level. This is in contrast to Maslow's claim in his masterwork, *Toward a Psychology of Being*, that the highest level of the human self is "self-actualization." Maslow's emphasis on the actualized self fails sociologically—human selves are built and sustained in constant relationships with each other.

In this and in the next chapters, we show that Miller's psychology of women unambiguously points us to The Sixth Level, and we identify the Core Differentiators that comprise The Sixth Level. These Core Differentiators are illustrated through our autobiographical cases and provide models of leadership that show that The Sixth Level is a better way—sustainable, productive, and healthy. There is much to learn from women's psychology. All of us, men and women, need to learn how to think it and how to do it![5]

How Patriarchy Persists in Daily Life

To understand the persistent causes of sexism, homophobia, and violence and what we are up against, we need to understand the structure, function, and processes of patriarchy[6] in which social structure and organization force social activities and social relationships to be male-dominated, male-identified, and male-centered (Johnson 1995). We also need to understand it does not need to be this way.

Patriarchy (Johnson 1995) is *male-dominated* insofar that it creates power differences between women and men based on gender alone. Men shape the culture to their own collective interests, such as drafting laws that favor men's rights over women's rights. For example, women in the United States got the vote in 1920, with great resistance, and 150 years after men. Patriarchy allows men to believe and assert their superiority over women, which results in men claiming that it is legitimate that they occupy favored social positions and that women occupy subordinate ones.

Patriarchy is *male-identified* insofar that it creates core cultural ideals about what is good, desirable, and preferable that are embedded in the masculine and not the feminine. For example, throughout the Third World, it is not uncommon that the birth of boys remains preferred over girls (resulting in the abortions of female embryos) or that wives are expected to be subordinate to their husbands.

Patriarchy is *male-centered* insofar that the focus of attention is primarily on men and their activities (Johnson 1995). It is not surprising that, almost universally, what is perceived as male work is rewarded more than perceived female work and that it is seen as more valued. It is not surprising that men tend to dominate conversations in public and are the focus when entertaining family guests. Patriarchy, in which men maintain power and privilege, justify these as rights because they provide production, protection, and procreation. Ironically, in the public sphere, male activity can range from leading other men to the most debased subordination by other men. But especially in relation to women, men are the dominators and women the subordinates.

Carol Gilligan and Naomi Snider, in *Why Does Patriarchy Persist?*, define patriarchy as:

A culture based on a gender binary and hierarchy, a framework or lens that:

1. Leads us to see human capacities as either "masculine" or "feminine" and to privilege the masculine.
2. Elevates some men over other men and all men over women.
3. Forces a split between the self and relationships so that in effect men have selves, whereas women are ideally self-less, and women have relationships, which surreptitiously serve men's needs. (2018, 6)

This last point is critical—the dominating forms of leadership split off self from relationship and ironically force women to be the relationship minders and keepers while exhibiting, as in *The Giving Tree*, self-sacrifice, self-denial, and subservience. At The Sixth Level, there is a toggling of self and relationship so that self is found in relationships and relationships allow for a more authentic and harmonious expression of self. This is what is meant by Self-in-Relation.

The Pain of Patriarchy and the Mask of Masculinity

When men follow the formulation of sexism, homophobia, and violence, when they enact it, it conceals our ability to think critically about the sexist model embedded in their masculinity. Sexism targets men as well as women, and it is sustained by threats by men toward other men! In the football metaphor, what appears to be a strong offense turns out to be a shaky defense, what appears to be security is a source of insecurity, and what appears to be confidence is often bluster, actually driven by fear.

Joseph Pleck has made it clear that there is a "paradox of power" in which, at one level, men's social identity is defined by the power they have over women and the power they compete for against other men. But at another level, *most men have very little power over their own lives* (Pleck 1981, 428). Thus, men exclude women, and selected other men, from their networks and their intimacies and escape into male fantasy behavior by which men keep their fears at bay, and by which men maintain their alleged security of male identity.

Utilizing the paradox of power as a model of how men experience their masculinity, we can begin to understand how men and women have also been disenfranchised by a hegemonic masculinity. It is apparent in any cursory observation that men in the United States, and other societies as well, are afraid of being ashamed, humiliated, or dominated by other men. It appears that as a group, men in patriarchies are trapped by the constant fear that "other men will unmask us, emasculate us, reveal to us and the world that we do not measure up, that we are not real men. We are afraid to let other men see that fear. Fear makes us ashamed, because the recognition of fear in ourselves is proof that we are not as manly as we pretend . . . our fear is the fear of humiliation" (Kimmel 1995, 131).

Men, whether in face-saving or ego-protecting cultures, shame cultures, or guilt cultures, reflect the paradox of power. But why should men give up the power and privilege they have? What is in it for them to do so? Men will not understand the real dynamics of sexism until they look at the *nature of how men oppress themselves*!

Men's dependence on an unequal power structure has created a "discontinuity between the social and the psychological." This has caused the efforts made by the women's movement to fall on deaf male ears. When confronted with the analysis that men have all the power, many men act incredulously: "What do you mean, men have all the power?" they ask. "What are you talking about? My wife bosses me around. My kids boss me around. My boss bosses me around. I have no power! I'm completely powerless!" (Kimmel 1995, 136). In their studies of men and masculinity, feminist theorists have wrongly assumed a "symmetry between the public and the private that does not conform to men's experiences" (Kimmel 1995, 136). In other words, men as a group in the public sphere have power, but in the private sphere they may feel "henpecked," "nagged," and "whipped." What has been missing from these analyses is a men's studies' perspective that seeks to understand *how men understand and experience themselves as part of "having to be a man" in society.* This would encourage a critical exchange between men and women, and men might realize how patriarchy has been a negative experience not only for women but also for most men.

There are two critically important aspects of manhood that provide us with insight.[7] The first is the observation that men experience emotional isolation, especially from other men, and are quite challenged to provide a good relationship for women. In friendships, in fraternities, and on teams, boys and men express identification with each other in so many ways, mainly instrumental (for example, talking about sports versus their personal feelings) but sometimes expressive.

In these men's worlds, they hope to find achievement and success (financial and otherwise), respect, and significant attachments to groups. Men enact many positive manly qualities, such as being courageous, determined, goal-oriented, hardworking, and selectively team-oriented. Boys and men hope to join a world where the models of men have been instrumental as inventors and industrious workers, happy providers, loyal husbands, and fathers. But in fact, most men in American culture have been followers and not leaders, as Thoreau says, living "lives of quiet desperation." This desperation has often resulted in acting out real social and psychological deprivations and experiencing the pain behind the mask of masculinity, including dissociating from feelings and acting out suppressed feelings in destructive behaviors such as alcoholism and domestic violence (Lynch and Kilmartin 1999).

American men are under a lot of pressure to conform to patriarchal demands: In the United States, suicide rates for women have been quite stable for over the past twenty years, while those for males, especially white male teenagers, have increased rapidly. Male teenagers are five times more likely to die by suicide than females. Overall, men are killing themselves at four times the rate of women. Men between the ages of eighteen and twenty-nine suffer alcohol dependency at three times the rate of women of the same age group. More than two-thirds of all alcoholics are men, and 50 percent more men are regular users of illicit drugs than women. Men account for more than 90 percent of arrests for alcohol and drug abuse violations. There is an increasing rate of unemployment among men, and of course, we know that men's life expectancy is 10 percent shorter than women's, often from stress-related heart disease and certain cancers. In other words, as Don Sabo has indicated in his work in men's studies, enacting American masculine behaviors can be dangerous to men's health (Messner 1992)! Ironically and unfortunately, there is a perception that these problems are caused by women gaining power. But the data has been consistent and persistent over time—it is not the result of feminism or the women's movement—these issues are embedded in patriarchy and the *oversocialization* of men to its demands.

Unfortunately success, respect, and group attachment are unequally distributed among men so that, for example, men of color often have less success, respect, and belonging than other groups of men. The striving for success is directly linked to stress and the high rate of cardiovascular disease among men. The striving for respect has often led to distorted images of other men through homophobic remarks and homophobic violence that render gay men victims of heterosexism, distorted images of women, and in men's sexualized violence toward women.

Finally, a great source of psychological distress for American men is loneliness. Often men simply fail to successfully attach themselves to groups that exercise satisfying emotional belonging. On the one hand, men desire male friendships that embody complete trust that other men will not take advantage of vulnerabilities. On the other hand, there are the competing demands of manhood to be the self-reliant loner, to be the winner, to be emotionally strong and hard, to be the rock. This makes it so difficult for men to approach each other with guards down. James L. Spates, writing about American "street games" (Spates 1976), argues that boyhood games teach men that the essence of manhood is competition. This becomes a code word for domination through physical force (wrestling, king of the hill, football), by emotional manipulation (name-calling and verbal cut games), or by acquiring more than the next fellow (read the automobile bumper sticker: "He who dies with the most toys, wins!"). This creates a model for men of manhood that can distort men's character and deprive them of significant friendships and more satisfying social relationships. This model of masculinity provides too few opportunities to expand the ethical and emotional lives of men.

Thus the second salient and related point: heterosexual men as a group are often a source of conflict, violence, substance abuse, and cruel sexist and sexual behavior. The acting out of deprivation and distortion has found itself principally in the use of violence against oneself and against others. That violence has many forms, including physical abuse of others, substance abuse, irresponsible sex, and risk-taking behavior. It has created a cycle of fear in women and a cycle of self-destruction in men.

Masculinity is a constant test, mainly around the theme of "the flight from the feminine (and the female)." This flight produces for men a very narrow bandwidth of acceptable experiences and relationships as men defend their so-called turf. A male student of Jack's declared, "I will take advantage of women as long as they let me." A group of young male university students in Jack's class derided and dismissed women's sports as uninteresting and amateurish because they did not exhibit the physical force and violence that these men felt had superior value. Efforts to encourage female achievement and equality in the face of male flight response from anything identified as female have resulted in many young men feeling deep betrayal, feeling that it is unfair that men should not be permitted to continue to dominate and be privileged because of their ascribed sex.

What do heterosexual men fear? Unable or unwilling to look carefully at masculinity itself, men deny that one of the significant themes of manhood is fear of other men. Simply, heterosexual men fear being exposed as a "sissy." Men pose a constant and relentless threat to each other so that throughout their lives, they fear being *unmasked as feminine*. The little tests of how men look at their hands and fingernails, of vocal inflection ("Do I sound gay or like a woman?"), of response to threats of violence ("Should I fight or do I run?")—every mannerism, every movement contains a coded gender language. In short, men fear other men, with whom each has to compete and seek to dominate, and for whom each performance is but a repeated test of manhood. This is the very foundation of sexism's double edge: if a man fails the tests, he risks being likened to the objects of our scorn and derision—females.

To be a man in most of the world is very problematic, and the demands of manhood, the roles that prove masculinity, are the root of men's insecurity, denial, and bluffing. Men must confront and enact change and expand beyond the male mystique of bluster, phoniness, and pretense, beyond talking the talk of sensitivity, beyond being politically correct (PC) in public and sexist and homophobic in private. And many men are ashamed of this behavior—but their *shame leads to silence*—so it appears that they actually approve of sexism, homophobia, and violence.

It is no surprise that college women often sadly relate that the male friend who treats them as an equal in private acts as a crude, sexist male in his male groups. This impulse to revert to the hegemonic and somewhat demonic image of the sexist male is rooted in male loyalty, not just to the men around them but to men as a general group. Men have difficulty changing without perceiving themselves as disloyal, a traitor to their sex. As a result, and in order to preserve this distorted male bond and social compact, men often resort to denial and distortion of themselves in defense of masculinity and especially the denial of the "other," mainly women, minorities, and homosexuals, discounting these groups' experiences and rendering them invisible.

But gender oppression and subordination are based on this lie—and deeply, viscerally, men know it is a lie. Women do not have equal pathways to succeed in the world. Women have a hard time winning. The sociologist Shur (1984) is unambiguous that women are caught in a double bind that labels them deviant. If they act within their own gendered boundaries, they are perceived as defective (not the normal—men). But if they adopt standard, Western, and usually white male behavior, they can be perceived as deviant "bitches." The subtext of male loyalty and the hidden texts of coded male behavior (for example, the male gaze, the wink or smirk) keep it so. Thus on the one hand, men together profess loyalty to this distorted ideal of masculinity, and simultaneously, because embedded in it is *fear of other men*, they find themselves in opposition to each other and to women.

The Sixth Level provides a social psychology that unties the gender knot (Johnson 1995) and frees everyone from the painful, destructive forms of gender scripting embedded in patriarchal systems. What might men learn from women about being a whole person, about living in the world differently, with more mental and physical health and more fruitful and healthier relationships? The Sixth Level provides men a way to full expression of their humanity and can vivify their relationships with women, their families, and their work and play places.

The Social and Historical Context for Change

Gender is a central fact in the distribution of power in virtually all societies. Educational, political, economic, social, familial, and other institutions are all gendered. The adherence to patriarchal ideology is maintained through consistent and unrelenting messaging and the concomitant threats against nonconforming men and women, as well as those who challenge the gender binary itself. Therefore, if we are to begin breaking down this gendered system, we must be cognizant that the essence of hegemonic masculinity exists to condemn variation. This includes differential valuation of people based on race, class, and other forms of human diversity. While gender is the main topic of this book, it is essential to recognize the multiplicative impact of race and class combined with gender, which amplifies each of these lines of oppression.

In the defense of the binary and the privilege it accords to men, men are expected to show loyalty by defending the gender distortions used to deny men's powerlessness in the face of other men. Fortunately we have gained more ground in the deconstruction of "gender laws" (and taken some steps backward) and are more aware of the problems presented by these "laws" and how essential it has become for the future of gender relations to change them. But this idea is not new, and the demonstration of the malleability of gender roles is most notable observed in Margaret Mead's work, *Sex and Temperament in Three Primitive Societies* (1935). In this work, Mead demonstrates through her ethnographies of three different tribes, the Arapesh (both sexes act like we conceptualize the feminine: gentle, nurturant, cooperative, and maternal), the Mundugumor (both the men and women are violent and aggressive and masculine), and Tchambuli (the woman are dominant and impersonal, and males are more passive and emotionally dependent), how flexible gender roles are. She calls for a renegotiation of gender roles in the United States, arguing that American social constructions of gender waste the broad talents of women.

Throughout human history, women's lives have been considered to be peripheral to the lives of men. As Boulding (1976) observes, the female world has more often than not been rendered invisible. The lives of most of the billions of women can be characterized as servitude, as sacrifice, and too often as suffering. Worldwide, there are significant differences in the life course of women and their varied conditions, and also the world of men. The world's women vary in life expectancy, scheduling of childbearing, childcare, and their household size. Men have a freedom of discretionary time that women do not. For women, it limits their degree of literacy and education (both very dangerous if rigid structures are the goal), and it constrains their degree of participation in nonhousehold activities. Reproduction and childcare sometimes take more and sometimes take less of the female life span.

But there is more to this "women's work" than meets the eye. Women create female networks and support systems that provide, out of love or duty, services to their families and the entire community that are integrative, centripetal, stabilizing, and conserving for the benefit of societies and their economies. Often these activities are about protection from harm, loss, or grief. What irony it is that women are socialized to be and act dependent, even helpless, in so many world cultures, and yet once married she must cater to the dependency of the man to whom she has been committed or to whom she has committed herself. Surely women have been and still are more economically dependent than men, institutional arrangements having forced them to be so.

Nevertheless, as Jessie Bernard has pointed out in her book, *The Future of Marriage* (1982), men are more often psychologically dependent on the wife, and it is men who benefit from being married, becoming quite dependent on their spouse's physical and emotional care for their well-being. The wife, reared to expect her dependency to be rewarded, finds herself in a position where she must fulfill the dependency needs of her husband but often enough finds her own needs unmet. Perhaps in some ancient time there was an authentic honoring of women and women's work. But women's household economies have since been rendered invisible. Since industrialization, productive activities are not considered by the powers that be to be work unless they are paid for. And while women are a valuable and crucial pool to the free market economy, they are undervalued as laborers and their household labor is not included in the GDP (gross domestic product) (Raworth, 2018). So working women take all the burdens—they sacrifice at home, and they sacrifice at work.

After studying the whole of human history, Boulding concludes that *women are the source of our solution to most of our human and social problems.* Under the historical leadership of men, we have had wars and conquest, the deterioration of the physical environment, and a disintegration of the social bond. Says Boulding:

> What will women make of the future? We have looked at the social maintenance, salvage, and repair work women have done since the beginning of urban civilization. Working mainly from the underside, the vast majority of them have continued to breed and rear children, hold households together, labor at economically productive work, and manage the grassroots level of redistribution of goods and services that has somehow held the polity together. All this they have done with and often without the aid of men. . . .

The design for disaster we currently face was not planned by women. They are absent from nearly all the decision-making bodies that have brought us where we are (Boulding 1976, 761).

The point is not that we should just let women lead but that men need to make room, learn how to lead more effectively with women's leadership as their model, or get out of the way. Our current condition, to echo Boulding, is historically the product of a male social psychology with its emphasis on domination, conflict, competition, individuation, and the subordination of women. The male bias in human knowledge has resulted in the denigration of female experience, the female perspective, and women's ways of leadership.

Thus women present a model of leading toward the future that has been right in front of our eyes, but we have so diminished its characteristics through the unequal relations of gender that we have not been able to see it and recognize its potential and power. It is embedded, as Jean Baker Miller reckons, in women's social psychology. We call it The Sixth Level. Says Boulding:

> ... Every woman with responsibility for a household is a practicing futurist. Families have traditionally depended on the capacity of mothers to hold in their minds the differently rhythmed developments of each person in a household as they age at their various rates through childhood, adolescence, middle years, and old age. Every family is a constellation of ever changing individuals, and is itself moving through successive stages of a family cycle, each stage with its own social, economic, and political requirements. Families would be in constant chaos if women did not have a grasp of futures and were not able to live mentally ahead of those around them. In fact, all human beings have that capacity. Women develop

it to a special degree because they have been given a larger share of the responsibility for family well-being (Boulding 1976, 781).

Such is the source of The Sixth Level.

Men and The Sixth Level Mindset

As Miller (1976) observes, Sixth Level leadership starts with women's embrace of mutuality, that critical sense of attachment and belonging that starts with family caretaking and that has been the social psychological domain of women. Relationships are at the core of women's interactions. It continues with the ingenious way women solve problems by imagining the future of others with whom they are in relationship and by working through or around male structures of domination. It requires a sense of justness to engage in behavior that is equitable. And finally, it results in a link between the leader and organizational members that makes the work worthwhile because the relationship is. The good news is that, as a social psychological phenomenon, it can be shared and learned by men as well.

There is hope: significant cohorts of the younger generation of women and men, millennials and Gen Zers, are less concerned about enforcing the binary and recognize a continuum and a fluidity of gender expression. They are uninterested in restricting social roles by gender. For example, these generations of men are demonstrating that they are better and more attentive parents than their fathers were, and a growing number of them are stay-at-home dads even as they risk challenges about their masculinity and work ethic (Crider 2020). The Sixth Level can guide men to stand against these distortions and false dichotomies, and men can express this new model, generating more positive and committed friendships and more enriching social relationships. Men can learn to foreground relationships—care for their partners, their children, and their employees—if we are to solve the problems of sexism, homophobia, and violence and enrich our organizations, businesses, and lives. There are several remarkable examples of groups and programs that are doing just this, focusing on boys and men learning how to care. Look at Equimundo, an international movement to help men be more effective care givers and fathers that is "promoting nurturing, non-violent, equitable masculinity since 2011" (www.equimundo.org/), and "Roots of Empathy" (www.rootsofempathy.org/), a project that has successfully introduced children into the ethic of care. Both projects, and many more, seek to help us to redefine a masculinity that is more inclusive and empathetic.

It is the special challenge of men today to develop as *gentle men*. Men can become better communicators and especially better listeners. Men can create groups and friendships that help them to feel secure in themselves so that they might truly be gentle men rather than exhibiting behavior that masks insecurity and vulnerability. Freed from a masculinity that puts men in the double bind of both loyalty and opposition to other men and the subordination of women, men will be able to unmask the self and be in an authentic relationship of care with women and with one another. New opportunities will become available, family and work relationships will be enhanced, and men's lives will be immeasurably enriched, more rounded, less lonely, and less stressful. Through new models of masculinity, men will find themselves becoming more active in their communities, doing good work, helping others, and acting as a source of great healing. This could lead to insights that could help men to be more receptive to change in personal relationships at home, structural and organizational arrangements at work, and gender norms and values that are part of the larger cultural matrix. And Gerson makes clear in her book, *The Unfinished*

Revolution (2011), that we will not be socially healthy until men adopt the shared responsibilities for childcare and the domestic household and women's public and private leadership is recognized and valued. To help with awareness, CoExist (www.getcoexist.com) created an app that gives domestic partners the platform to go beyond mere lists and creates equity in domestic activities.

Of course, the need is broader than just the transformation of gender relations. As a theory and a process, Self-in-Relation inevitably requires us to consider the complex intersectionalities[8] that many people experience. For example, bell hooks (1984) critiques the white women's movement insofar that it failed to recognize and include the experience of black women (as Sojourner Truth laments, *Ain't I A Woman?* [1851]) and by doing so ignored the more inclusive and essential changes that are necessary for achieving broader equity and equality. The Sixth Level, based in Self-in-Relation, requires a holistic awareness of the array of relationships that are reflective of human diversity and variation.

This Sixth Level integrates men as partners in a movement for social change that seeks expanded leadership roles for women and others who have been disenfranchised in all sectors of the society. It recognizes the value of expanded roles for men in family life in which men are truly partners, critical participants in solving current gender and social problems. The necessary elements that constitute gender equity are illustrated in Figure 4 (The Radial of Gender Equity). It is a path to human integrity that embraces the mutual recognition and empathy of those we love and those with whom we live and work. It will transform our organizational and business structures into more sustainable, productive, and profitable enterprises. It draws not only on goodwill but keen self-interest. Who would choose to live otherwise?

FIGURE 4. THE RADIAL OF GENDER EQUITY

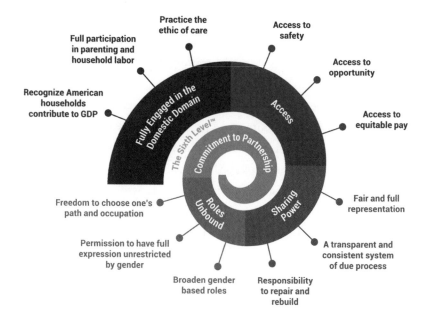

However, do not underestimate the power and persistence of patriarchy. The sexism of patriarchy forces disconnection between not only women and men but between men themselves. The mask of masculinity distorts ourselves and our relationships. As you will see, The Sixth Level is distinguished by its rejection of forms of leadership that are derived from patriarchy. It asserts that women's long-standing model of leadership, derided and dismissed as too emotional, too weak, too much engaged in relationships, and unproductive, is just the kind of leadership that humans require to thrive and to be sustainably productive. The data makes this very apparent. Simply put, as you will see in the cases by women leaders that follow, Sixth Level leadership works.

CHAPTER 3

The Irony in the Awakening: Emotions and Leadership

"One of the criticisms I've faced over the years is that I'm not aggressive enough or assertive enough, or maybe somehow, because I'm empathetic, it means I'm weak. I totally rebel against that. I refuse to believe that you can't be both compassionate and strong."

—Jacinda Ardern, prime minister of New Zealand from 2017 to 2023

Emotions Denied!

In 1971 President Nixon stated in a conversation with Attorney General John N. Mitchell, "I don't think a woman should be in any government job whatever. I mean, I really don't. The reason why I do is mainly because they are erratic. And emotional."[1]

Nixon was not alone in his belief that women are too emotional to hold high-level leadership positions. Indeed, in 2013, the cover of *Harvard Business Review* featured a story on the "biases that hold female leaders back," with a silhouette of a woman and only three phrases in large, boldface type: 'Too Nice,' 'Bossy,' 'Emotional.'"[2]

Emotions expressed by women have historically been criticized as signs of weakness or immaturity, and women's pursuit of emotional connection has been similarly viewed as a deficiency. Women's needs, therefore, run counter to the conventional ideal image of leaders who are admired for their independence and self-reliance. This bias has resulted in high-level leadership positions being out of reach for most women.

Emotions Awakened

However, while Nixon and many others were denigrating women as emotional Jean Baker Miller was revolutionizing the study of psychology. In 1976 she turned the notion of the superiority of independence upside down. In *Toward a New Psychology of Women*, Miller not only argued that women's psychological development and their ability to create and sustain relationships may differ from men's, but emotional and social connections are more important than individuation for all people. In Miller's formulation, the fully realized self needs mutuality.

During the same era, modern leadership theory began to spotlight emotions. These theories focused on "the complex interactions among the leader, the followers, the situation, and the system as a whole."[3] Transformational leadership theories, in which leaders encourage, inspire, and motivate, began to flourish.[4] One of the more renowned leadership theories emerged in 1970 when Robert K. Greenleaf wrote *The Servant as Leader*. He asserted that the best leaders are those concerned with others. He asked, "Do those served grow as persons? Do they, while being served, become healthier, wiser, freer, more autonomous, more likely themselves to become servants?"[5] The implication was that leaders are obliged to care about the emotional well-being of those they lead.

Fast forward to one of the most noteworthy leadership theories of the modern era—Emotional Intelligence Theory. In 1995, Daniel Goleman published the book *Emotional Intelligence,* and it became a

New York Times, as well as an overseas, bestseller. He defined emotional intelligence as self-awareness, self-regulation, empathy, and social skill.[6] He explained that a leader may have smart ideas, but without emotional intelligence, their ideas would likely not translate into action, as leaders need others to carry out their ideas. A few years later, in 2001, Goleman, Richard Boyatzis, and Annie McKee further developed the idea of emotional intelligence in the workplace with their groundbreaking book *Primal Leadership*. This book advanced Goleman's thesis that emotional intelligence is crucial to strong leadership and examined the role of emotions in motivating a workforce to achieve great results. *Primal Leadership* asserted that empirical and neuroscience research indicates emotions are contagious. Therefore, leaders' own emotions and their ability to manage them, in addition to their social awareness and ability to manage relationships, influence the success of an organization. Effective leaders "prime good feeling in those they lead,"[7] moving people to perform at their highest level.

The focus on emotions and relationships in these modern leadership theories addresses the complexity resulting from globalization, rapidly changing technology, and other changes in the trade environment. An organization's greatest asset in meeting these changes is the ability to access, process, and exchange information while maintaining the products and processes currently in use.[8] Thus, collaboration between individuals, teams, and departments is paramount, and understanding and communicating emotions is the engine for creating these relationships.

Toward a New Leadership Mindset

In an economy that is dependent on collaboration and innovation leaders must be skilled in developing and supporting relationships. A social psychology favoring relationships is even more critical in such an economy. However, as explained in Chapters 1 and 2, the social psychological framework that emerges from a patriarchal system promotes individualism and self-reliance rather than connection and relationships. There is a disconnect between the psychological mindset driven by patriarchy and the mindset needed to survive in today's, and conceivably tomorrow's, economic environment.

Self-in-Relation theory,[9] with an emphasis on connection and relationships, suggests a social psychological paradigm that takes us from a conventional mindset based on patriarchy to a mindset needed for profitability in today's marketplace. Indeed, Self-in-Relation theory was developed to provide a psychological framework to fit women's relational experiences. Its chief principle of growing in connection with others can also serve as a foundation for leaders who wish to prioritize relationships within organizations.

As stated in Chapter 1, Self-in-Relation theory was conceptualized by the founders of the Stone Center at Wellesley College, an organization founded in 1984 with Dr. Jean Baker Miller as its director. One of its missions was to house the writings of Dr. Miller, Dr. Judith Jordan, Dr. Irene Stiver, Dr. Janet Surrey, and others. These scholars developed psychological theories that "break free from what they felt were the damaging effects for women of traditional therapy."[10] Their Self-in-Relation theory suggests that women must be viewed in context with their social environment and the influence of the patriarchal system. Accordingly, women's patterns of behaviors, attitudes, and beliefs reflect their roles as caretakers and helpers. Consequently, as women have developed in relation to others, they have learned to connect emotionally and support one another. As Surrey explained, Self-in-Relation marks a departure from over one hundred years of developmental theory that prioritizes separation over connection. She stated:

The notion of Self-in-Relation involves an important shift in emphasis from separation to relationship as the basis for self-experience and development. Further, relationship is seen as the basic goal of development: that is, the deepening capacity for relationship and relational competence . . . Other aspects of self-development emerge in the context of relationship, and there is no inherent need to disconnect or sacrifice relationships for self-development.[11]

We argue that Self-in-Relation Theory offers a social psychological framework that is a necessary precursor to leadership theories and models that prioritize relationships.

An examination of the two current well-known leadership theories mentioned earlier, Emotional Intelligence and servant leadership, through the lens of Self-in-Relation Theory, reveals an invisible yet powerful and overarching influence of social psychology on leadership skills.

Before introducing this analysis, it is important to note two principles. First, this discussion generalizes women's relational behaviors and thought processes. In fact, there is a continuum of women (as well as men) who are relationship oriented; and there are women who are more individualistic. However, generalizations reflect social norms and help to project likely outcomes. They help us make sense of noticeable trends and are therefore useful in exploring the impact of social psychological theory on leadership.

Second, while it is beyond the scope of this book to examine all aspects of emotional intelligence or servant leadership, two components that are common to both theories, relationships and empathy illustrate the value of Self-in-Relation as a foundational theory for modern leadership.

Relationships and Leadership through the Lens of Self-in-Relation Theory

Relationships are central to Emotional Intelligence (EI) and servant leadership. EI is defined as "how leaders handle themselves and their relationships."[12] The theory asserts that an emotional bond between leaders and employees motivates people to "share ideas, learn from one another, make decisions collaboratively, and get things done."[13] There are four skills or domains that compose EI: self-awareness, self-management, social awareness, and relationship management.[14] *All require understanding oneself in relation to others.*

Goleman et al. explained, "Reading one's own emotions and recognizing their impact"[15] (self-awareness) are fundamental to forming relationships. So too is the ability to manage one's emotions.[16] While positive emotions such as enthusiasm do not require much control, "No leader can afford to be controlled by negative emotions, such as frustration and rage,"[17] when interacting with others. EI also requires social awareness, or the ability to "read another person's face and voice."[18] This skill helps people "harmonize their emotional state,"[19] or create resonance. Resonance helps leaders "move a crowd," or motivate people to unite around a common goal.[20] Finally, Goleman et al. contended that when these three skills come together, they help leaders manage relationships and perform leadership functions such as persuading others, resolving conflict, and collaborating.[21] Thus, EI highlights the emotional interplay between self and others in forming relationships that affect productivity, the organizational leader's chief objective.

Similar to EI, relationships are the centerpiece of servant leadership theory. Servant leaders are stewards who develop and empower others through trusting relationships that are characterized by the leaders' capacity to astutely interpret others' emotions, concerns, and behaviors.[22]

Relationship skills can be learned, as revealed by Goleman et al., who provide several persuasive examples of leaders who have acquired relational leadership skills. However, while teaching relationship skills is needed, Self-in-Relation suggests that women have been learning and practicing the interplay between the self and others all their lives. By the time they become leaders, they are seasoned relationship managers.

The Stone Center scholars observed that from the moment of birth, the "self" is in active emotional connection with the mother or caretaker. Miller explained, "In this sense, the infant, actively exerting an effect on the relationship, begins to develop an internal sense of itself as one who changes the emotional interplay for both participants."[23] In other words, emotions are a language used between infant and caretaker, and both are changed by these wordless exchanges.

More often than boys, as girls mature, they are encouraged to "augment their abilities to 'feel as the other feels' and to practice 'learning about the other.'"[24] Jordan explained that for girls, "The movement into and out of connection becomes a journey of discovery about self, other, and relationship . . . The importance of connectedness is affirmed, and one's capacity to move into healthy connection is strengthened."[25]

As girls continue to develop relationship skills into childhood and beyond, they attain relational competence, or "the capacity to move another person, to effect change in a relationship, or affect the well-being of all participants."[26] Hence, when they become leaders, they have already cultivated the building blocks of relational interactions.

Empathy and Leadership through the Lens of Self-in-Relation Theory

The *Oxford English Dictionary* defines *empathy* as "the ability to understand and share the feelings of another."[27] In addition to relationship skills, empathy is a central component of EI and servant leadership. Goleman et al. explain, "All leadership includes this primal dimension."[28] According to EI, empathy enables a leader to respond appropriately to employees' concerns and helps form relationships. Empathetic leaders can "calm fears, assuage anger, or join in good spirits," thereby forming positive relationships.[29] Servant leadership also relies on leaders' ability to be empathetic. It asserts that leaders have a responsibility to learn about their followers' needs and aspirations, as well as to share in their pain and frustrations. Empathy helps servant leaders "determine how best to serve their [followers'] needs."[30]

While it may seem contradictory, the traditional role of caretaker, which implies a subordinate role, helps women become better leaders, as caretaking is a source of opportunities for developing empathy. Caring for and nurturing others contributes to the mental constructions that facilitate mutual empathy in both girls and women. Girls begin to develop empathy as they engage with their mother, becoming attuned to their mother's "feeling state" and having conversations that include "emotional sharing."[31] As girls mature, they continue to share feelings and "see through the eyes of others"[32] when interacting with friends, family, and other members of their community.

The value of lifelong practice in developing empathy can be understood by examining how the brain processes empathy. Empathy is not a simple behavior and is developed over time. Jordan explains that empathy involves "complex cognitive and affective interactions. "[33] She describes affective interactions as "feelings of emotional connectedness" that allow one to "fully take in and contain the feelings of the other person."[34] Cognitive interactions refer to the ability to maintain a sense of self while simultaneously feeling connected.[35] Jordan postulated empathy is complex because it involves holding on to two opposing thoughts at the same time: emotional connectedness and one's own individuality.[36] She suggested the brain is trained to perform this task through extensive practice.[37]

Another Stone Center scholar, Alexandra G. Kaplan, confirmed Jordan's hypothesis that "women are schooled in empathy throughout their lives, including this coexistence of seemingly contradictory positions."[38] Surrey added that the evolving process of growing in relation to others is a two-way interactional process that involves feeling as well as understanding, thus preparing girls to be empathetic.[39]

Toggling

The Stone Center's hypothesis that empathy is made up of complex mental interactions is supported by recent neuroscience research. In *Helping People Change*, Boyatzis, Smith, and Van Oosten (2019) reported that Dr. Helen Reiss's work in the field of neuroscience has revealed three different "facets" of empathy—cognitive, emotional, and behavioral.[40] They explain, "Cognitive empathy involves conceptually understanding the perspective of another person and draws on the neural networks that involve analytical processing."[41] Emotional empathy is "the ability to be emotionally in tune with another person and feel what she feels."[42] Behavioral empathy is "the motivation to help another person in some way."[43]

The similarities between the Stone Center's model of empathy, written in 1991, and recent findings in neuroscience are striking. Both suggest two different parts of the brain, one activated by emotions and the other activated by cognitions, work together to enable an individual to be empathetic. However, what is most compelling about a comparison between the Stone Center's model of empathy and recent findings in neuroscience is the suggestion that empathy is developed through practice.[44]

Helping People Change also reports on the work of neuroscientist, Anthony Jack and his colleagues, who studied the brain's two neural networks—the "empathic network" [45] and the "analytical network"[46] (see Figure 5: The Toggle). The empathic network is activated by emotions, and the analytical network relates to tasks and problem-solving.[47] Surprisingly, Jack et al. found that the two neural networks work in opposition to each other. They are antagonistic.[48] That is, when one network is in use, the other is suppressed.[49] The brain actively toggles, or moves back and forth, between the two networks.[50] Those who are balanced in their use of both networks toggle more fluidly.[51] Thus, as the Stone Center's model concludes that empathy requires practice, the model of Anthony Jack and his colleagues suggests that repetition trains the two opposing neural networks to toggle fluidly, and perhaps more quickly, between empathy and analysis.[52]

FIGURE 5. THE TOGGLE

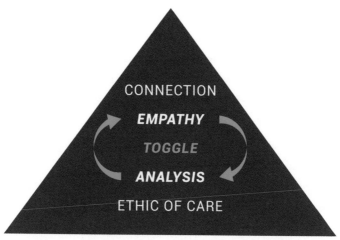

CONNECTION
EMPATHY
TOGGLE
ANALYSIS
ETHIC OF CARE

The Sixth Level™

Women's traditional roles as caretakers and helpers impel them to practice empathy as well as analysis while young, and in turn prepares them for leadership as adults who can toggle fluidly. Consequently, Self-in-Relation Theory exposes the myth that women are too emotional for leadership in the workplace. Emotions are the foundation of relationships in EI and servant leadership, two preeminent leadership theories that illustrate the need for relational skills. Self-in-Relation asserts that throughout their lives, women strive to understand and to be understood and to empower and be empowered.[53] They embody the relational skills that lead to organizational success.

Implications for Practice

This discussion of EI and servant leadership, framed by Self-in-Relation theory, suggests three important points: first, men's mindsets would be enhanced by developing empathic skills within a relational framework of development, such as Self-in-Relation. Second, more women are needed to bring empathic relationship skills to the highest echelons of leadership. Third, the most effective leadership requires toggling between the empathic and the analytic networks.[54]

1. Miller's book, *Toward a New Psychology of Women* (1976), was written in response to women being misdiagnosed and maligned by psychological theories that were based on men[55] and the notion that independence and self-reliance are the sine qua non of a healthy psychology.[56] Ironically, psychological theories that support men's separation and individuation, imply limits to men's leadership skills in the current economic environment. As Miller explained, "American theorists of early psychological development and, indeed, of the entire life span,

from Erik Erikson (1950) to Daniel Levinson (1978), tend to see all of development as a process of separating oneself out from the matrix of others—'becoming one's own man.'"[57] Consequently, when men raised in this framework try to become relational leaders, they find themselves being asked to do something very different from all their prior development.[58] Men may therefore resist adopting relational behaviors as they are inconsistent with the image of a strong, independent leader. As explained in Chapter 2, men may fear being labeled a "sissy" if they reject this conventional image of masculinity and become more focused on relationships. Furthermore, since relational skills like empathy involve practice, men who are encouraged to develop empathy may be reluctant to complete the hard work required and may therefore remain relationship deficient. Hence, many men may benefit from exposure to research on the advantages of relational skills in the workplace and at home. Encouraging them to participate in training to develop relational skills will help them become better leaders and partners. Including Self-in-Relation theory in their training would empower them to shift to a mindset where relational skills are prioritized.

2. Today, even after the value of relational leadership has been supported in numerous studies, only 10.4 percent of Fortune 500 CEOs are women.[59] There is an obvious gap between theory and practice. This suggests that despite the burgeoning research on women's psychological strengths and how they translate into leadership strengths, women are still often undervalued and underutilized. While there are more women leaders than there were twenty years ago, the

pace needs to accelerate for businesses to benefit from more relational leadership. As presented in previous chapters of this book, Self-in-Relation presents an alternative to the norms and social psychology that underly the patriarchal belief system.

3. Self-in-Relation, a social psychological framework that women have developed to survive in a patriarchal system, serves to empower both men and women. This framework of growing in connection, rather than separating from others, encourages toggling between empathic and analytical processes.

Conclusion

Growing evidence of the importance of awareness and the understanding of emotions in the workplace has awakened leaders and scholars during the last half century. Ironically, women continue to be excluded from leadership because they are believed to be too emotional and relationship-oriented. But there is another irony in the gap between valued leadership skills such as emotional intelligence and empathy, and the social psychology embedded in our patriarchal system. The roles assigned to women and men under patriarchy allow women to develop these important leadership qualifications more than men. Breaching the bounds of patriarchy can therefore be helpful to both men and women and valuable for social and business success. It will open the gates to allow more women into top leadership ranks. It will also enable men to be more emotionally intelligent and to develop stronger relationships. Men will become better leaders and as discussed in Chapter 2, it would help men lead more meaningful lives. (See Figure 4).

Emerging Leaders

CHAPTER 4
Reflections and Expectations of Emerging Leaders

WE INVITED TWO EMERGING leaders to share their stories and insights because we were curious about what this generation seeks in its leaders. We speculated that emerging leaders would not be able to find novel solutions for the unprecedented challenges facing most leaders today. Kirby Gilmore was recommended by Dr. Rachel Talton who was Kirby's mentor and a contributor. Sam Allen was recommended by Dr. Jack Harris who was his professor and author.

We asked the emerging leaders to "share an experience where you worked in a dissonant environment that prevented you from doing your best work or made you feel that you wanted out. What did the leader(s) do to create such an environment? Was the leader dismissive, dictatorial, harsh, or discouraging? Please give an example."

We gave them two choices: "envision what you would want from a leader. Describe the traits or actions of a leader that would help you succeed. Imagine an example that illustrates how a leader could create an environment that encourages your best work;" OR "compare your negative experience to one where you got what you needed from a leader. Did the leader motivate, encourage, or push you in a positive way? What did they do that helped you? Please provide an example."

CHAPTER 4

Reflections and Expectations of Emerging Leaders

Leadership Dreams Can Come True

By Kirby Gilmore

BEING A WOMAN BORN in the 2000s, my first introduction to strong female leadership was through *The Powerpuff Girls* television show.

The name may sound frivolous, but this animated television series, launched in 1998, depicted a diverse group of powerful women leaders. Furthermore, the show offered an interesting comparison between public interest in women leaders and their private struggle to prove their strength and worth.

The three main Powerpuff characters, Blossom, Bubbles, and Buttercup, had extraordinary skills that they used to battle evil and save the inhabitants of the City of Townsville from a variety of nefarious characters. They were superheroes, leading the charge without needing help from anyone. They showed children all over the world that women of any age can be powerful and effective leaders.

As I watched *The Powerpuff Girls* as a young girl, I drew these important lessons:

- Female leaders are viable sources of power in the world.
- Young women can achieve great things when they put their minds and hearts into challenges they face.
- Female leadership emphasizes inclusion, which creates positive, growth-oriented environments.

As a young child, I decided this was the kind of leader I wanted to be—a leader who rises in the ranks of the workforce like Blossom, rallies those around her, checks on the people she cares about, and demonstrates strength against impossible odds.

Then I entered the workforce and discovered a different ambiance. Not everyone believes Powerpuff principles, and not every leader operates with the same values and leadership skills as my heroes.

I found a job on campus when I was getting my master's degree, and I was excited to earn enough money to cover my expenses. I was also eager for the chance to get more plugged in to my university, learning about available resources and forming relationships campus-wide. When I interviewed, I mentioned that I was in the school's graduate program and that my orientation schedule conflicted with the mandatory job training. I was assured by my new boss that the scheduling conflict would not create a problem. However, when the first scheduling conflict occurred, the warm, accommodating response I had received when I was hired turned disapproving and dismissive.

I was taken aback. I believed I had been proactive in getting approval to miss some training sessions. But in an about-face, my supervisor gave me what seemed like an ultimatum—either I attended all the job training events or I would find myself out of a job.

I considered resigning. I believed it would be better to go sooner rather than later if this was the kind of treatment I could expect. Before deciding, however, I went up the chain of command and talked to the department chair. He essentially affirmed the original accommodation and assured me that I could attend my school's orientation and review my job training materials during my personal time.

The next day, my supervisor apologized and said that she would work with my schedule. I felt great relief, but it turned out to be the start of strained dynamics between me and my supervisor. In one-on-one meetings, my supervisor acted as though we were a team, but in staff meetings, she reneged on the plans we had developed together. She set a pattern of being alternately nice and extremely stern, giving me creative autonomy and then taking it away.

I found myself trying to limit our interactions as much as possible, and in the absence of my supervisor's support, I leaned on my network to help me find ways to contribute. Unfortunately, I still found myself holding back, not speaking up during department meetings for fear of backlash.

This was not the strong, assertive leadership I had seen in *The Powerpuff Girls*. It was a suffocating environment where emerging leaders were squashed. Nevertheless, I remained resilient and called on my memories of the strong Powerpuff Girls to keep me on track.

At the end of the year, my supervisor was assigned to another department, and I had a fresh start with a new leader. I was glad that I had stayed positive and made choices that kept me open to new opportunities. Now, with a little space to reflect, it occurred to me that my former supervisor's leadership style had kept me from showing up the way I wanted to. I promised myself that as I progressed in my career, I would look for leaders who are trustworthy, inspiring, and supportive. I could see myself thriving in environments where leaders display kindness and take the time to ask, "Is everything okay?"

When I entered Case Western Reserve University, it was my good fortune to find a leader such as I had envisioned. Dr. Rachel Talton became my mentor and demonstrated the qualities I remembered admiring as a child. She insisted that I excel, find my voice, and take chances on myself.

People can be divided into two categories: dream builders and dream killers. Dr. Talton is a dream builder. She pays close attention to nuances in what you say, and she cares deeply about your circumstances. She expects a lot of herself too—to be a good servant and set a positive example. I needed a leader who would reach out and show me how to enhance my reputation, credentials, and self-worth. And not just me; my generation is seeking leaders we can look up to and who will guide us to exceed our own expectations and make the world a better place.

Now, within the pages of this book, *The Sixth Level*, all of us have access to narratives from women leaders, including Dr. Talton, that illustrate strategies and qualities that can help us become the kind of leaders that we must be.

Getting Back in the Game

By Sam Allen

OUR COACH DRAGGED THE metal chair into the center of the court as we all looked at each other in confusion and exhaustion. He ordered my teammate to sit there and then told the rest of us to run baseline-to-baseline sprints as he watched until we literally couldn't run another step. We'd already finished a grueling practice session, but we were being made to suffer in front of him because my teammate had committed an unpardonable mistake:

He'd arrived late to practice because of a family emergency.

That kind of leadership, that singling out of individual players for a minor error with the explicit goal of inducing shame and guilt, was what I had seen a hundred times with male coaches. It had no productive basis and was yet another contributor to a dissonant environment that severely limited both individual and team success. In fact, by that point, the coach's leadership style had made me want to quit playing the sport I had once loved. Just as I was coming to terms with the fact that my love for basketball had disappeared, a new coach stepped in and brought forth a change of culture that reinvigorated my passion for the sport.

The second coach showed me a special kind of leadership I'd never encountered before. He brought in relationship building, ingenuity, celebration of the individual, team camaraderie, and an emphasis on the players being more important than the score on the board. He was hard on us when he needed to be but never domineering or cruel. He built a culture around the pillars of pride, unity, respect, multiple efforts, and the concept of things being "bigger than basketball." As I studied the sociology of leadership in the college classroom, it was fascinating to see the theoretical principles of effective leadership play out anecdotally in my day-to-day experiences.

When I was asked to be a part of this book, I thought that, as a man, I wouldn't have anything to add to the conversation. However, my studies and my firsthand experiences have reinforced the principles of The Sixth Level over and over again: achieving results doesn't require the use of a dictatorial leadership style. In fact, such toxic leadership styles actually undermine organizational and individual success. You don't have to pound people into submission or humiliate them in the middle of a basketball court. You can create an environment that gets them to buy in, develops a positive culture, and makes every teammate intrinsically motivated to perform well.

Until that second coach, all I'd seen in my life was the stereotypical leadership approach: Dominate. Attack. Crush your opponent. That attitude is commonplace in the world of sports, particularly male sports, where a certain level of aggression is demanded—and admittedly, sometimes needed—to pursue the ultimate objective of winning competitions. Particularly violent and aggressive sports such as American football take this a step further by employing terminology derived from warfare: sending a blitz, throwing a bomb, dominating the trenches.

While effort and intensity are bedrock qualities of any high-performing athlete and/or team, on the field or in the office, success depends equally on effective teamwork, communication, and an understanding of how others will act and react to particular environments and situations. The aggression that can win a championship can tear an organization apart if it isn't fostered in an inclusive, empowering environment.

That hasn't been the style of choice for many leaders who approach the workplace the same as my first coach had, who at one point explicitly told us: "Each and every one of you is under constant evaluation." That line has never left my memory because of the sheer anxiety and panic it instilled in my then nineteen-year-old self. Now, seven years removed from that moment, it seems absurd—a grown adult telling a group of eighteen- to twenty-one-year-old kids that not only were their in-game performances being assessed, but every play of every practice was being filmed, reviewed, and dissected with the sole purpose of finding the slightest lapse in technique or effort. To us, his comment was understood as: "I will see any mistake you make, and you will be punished for it."

That created a collective fear of making mistakes among the team. In the game of basketball, creativity is key—when a team or player plays in a predictable fashion, the opposing team is able to plan for and prepare for that probability. We were all so terrified to make a mistake (and end up publicly berated or pulled out of the game) that we did everything we could to avoid errors of any kind. Stripped of the confidence and empowerment necessary to grow and improve, the culture in which we operated had the unfortunate effect of inhibiting our development as players, preventing our team from reaching its full potential.

This environment also intentionally pitted teammates against each other, which only bred resentment and fractured the necessary bonding all teams need to succeed. While there are practical constraints in the sport (games are finitely 40 minutes long, only five players can share the court at one time), this culture fostered the belief that any one teammate's advancement in playing time or status was inherently a penalty or punishment of another player. Our coach applauded this dog-eat-dog approach even though it was slowly tearing apart our team's morale and confidence.

My experience within this culture, though it was grueling, taught me important lessons about the power of leadership, and the qualities of effective leaders. The common tropes around leadership—to always act like you know everything and are always right—don't actually work well in the long run. You can build sustainable success by being honest and vulnerable, by working with your team from a relationship standpoint rather than a place of dominance. I think a lot of the problems we have today, in organizations and in our society, are due to this emphasis on toxicity. If we can get beyond that and embrace a new form of leadership, we can create better organizations, and more importantly, better human beings.

Our new coach took a humans-first approach, and it made a massive difference not only in our team's confidence but in each of us young men as individuals. That tone was set by our first team-sanctioned activity: a tour of our coach's hometown, including his childhood home, the basketball court he played on as a child, and his grandparents' home. The day culminated in a cookout shared between his family and our team. The objective of the day wasn't to get us to run wind sprints or to become more aggressive on the court. It was simply to give the team an understanding of what had shaped him into the person he had become and to build genuine connections with his players beyond the game of basketball. The coach built a culture around the prioritization of personal connections and genuine care for everyone within the program.

This emphasis on personal connection continued throughout the season. We had a "lifeline" series in which teammates and coaches paired up (sometimes even across levels of authority in player-coach pairings) and told each other stories about our upbringings, major life events, values, and the life lessons we had learned. These stories were deeply personal and emotional, and even though sometimes the time spent telling them strained the schedules we were all attempting to balance, they proved to be invaluable in fostering a culture in which we all understood, cared for, and valued one another.

I know this because to this day, a special and genuine connection exists between each and every member of that team. Even though it has been four years since our time as "teammates" ended, the level of communication and strength of relationships between members in this group remains strong, which is a rare dynamic.

This new type of leadership style we experienced not only built a healthy culture in the locker room, but it led to stellar results for our team. In the one season I played under the new coach, we were viewed externally as a team with mediocre talent and picked to finish as an average team in our league. We exceeded everyone's expectations, even our own, and had the most successful season in the school's history – culminating by becoming the first team in school history to win multiple games in the prestigious NCAA championship tournament. That coach, and the experience of that special season, left an impact on our school and on every single one of us.

The best leaders are people who demonstrate a sincere concern for those they lead. They don't act as if they are above any individual, and through both actions and words, they develop relationships with and genuinely care for everyone within their organization. These kinds of leaders inspire followers to bring their authentic selves and best efforts to their endeavors, and they spur intrinsically motivated success. These are the kinds of leaders in the pages of this book and the kinds of people who will take the rest of us through any crisis with a keen sense of concern for others and the collective well-being. They are the kinds of leaders who build a culture where everyone wants to give their best—and always make sure no one ever feels driven off the court.

Case Studies of Sixth Level Leadership

Introduction to Section 3

Discoveries made through an examination of leadership theories and Self-in-Relation speak to a need for more information about women's leadership skills and attributes. In the next four chapters, sixteen women leaders share their leadership stories. While their narratives demonstrate relational styles similar to emotional intelligence and servant leadership, they reveal new insights and attributes. Moreover, they all reflect the foundational theory of Self-in-Relation. Thus, the new Sixth Level model expands the old, incomplete model that prematurely ends with self-actualization—Maslow's hierarchy of needs. Now, Self-in-Relation sits atop Maslow's pyramid as The Sixth Level, indicating that learning about oneself in relation to others is the most evolved developmental stage.

As discussed in Chapter 1, the four Core Differentiators that emerge from the Self-in-Relation umbrella are mutuality, ingenuity, justness, and intrinsic motivation. While the narratives frequently reflect more than one Core Differentiator, each chapter highlights and illustrates one salient differentiator.

The narratives also show that Sixth Level leadership delivers positive results. These leaders have achieved profitability and sustainability by fostering relational cultures. Combined, there are $18 billion in revenue and over 45,000 employees represented. This demonstrates that business success can be achieved in organizations where leaders use the four Core Differentiators and toggle between the empathic and the analytic (Boyatzis, Rochford, and Jack 2015).

In these compelling narratives, you will find bold, creative, inspiring, and caring leaders. They solve problems, discover opportunities, and respond to opportunities while balancing the needs of the organization with the needs of stakeholders. Importantly, these narratives provide evidence of what is possible when women have the chance to demonstrate their skills and dedication to success. Moreover, they illustrate what the workplace looks like when guided by The Sixth Level.

CHAPTER 5

Mutuality: The Critical Importance of Connection

CHAPTER 1 DESCRIBES THIS Core Differentiator, mutuality, as the ability to engender an emotional connection between two people where there is genuine exchange of "experiencing each other" and "influencing each other"—think of it as mutual empathy where concern flows both ways.

Mutuality builds a culture of community in organizations through seeking out input and opinions from those we trust. It is about treating the organization you lead as a living organism. Sixth Level leaders view the organization as an organism they are responsible for cultivating, curating, and nurturing. This type of connectivity means having a relationship with both the individuals and the entity itself.

THE CORE DIFFERENTIATORS

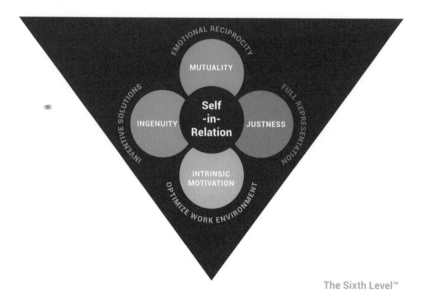

The Sixth Level™

Great Collaborations

By Karen Grasso

IT WAS THE MOST stressful time, and then it was the most successful time. While at first it seemed the odds were against us, momentum that had been carefully cultivated and built from a culture fueled by trust, caring, and purpose carried my team to satisfying success. I began building this team culture immediately upon taking office as Business Unit President, and it was exciting to experience the results of our hard work.

In our business, when a long-term client sends out requests for proposals (RFP) to the entire marketplace, it can feel very personal as well as threatening. It is a necessary practice, as our clients must determine if our team continues to be the best fit. But RFPs trigger strong emotions and require a massive effort from our people. When this happens, I remind our team that retention efforts are like winning the client for the first time—again and again. I encourage them to see the process as an opportunity to refresh our practices, review our successes as partners, and demonstrate our value proposition. In the end, this process enhances our relationships and connections with our clients.

After working with our company for fifteen years, one of our clients sent out an RFP and invited six companies to compete for their contract. The pressure for us to succeed was intense. Our competitors undercut our prices, plus our client had a relationship with one of the competing companies. We almost always feel like the underdog in these situations, but we had a secret weapon. The work we had been doing to develop a new corporate culture gave us a competitive advantage.

Before I became president of the business unit, the work culture in our office had deteriorated. An overarching sense of uncertainty had prevailed, and morale was low. Few initiatives were being undertaken, employees worked in silos, and they came and left at their own discretion. I knew I needed to reconstruct the culture.

As I began my new role, I gathered my team together and explained how I intended to lead. I said, "I want our team to pull together, learn to trust one another, and be transparent with each other. In addition, I am going to hold you accountable. In exchange, I am going to be accountable to you and will share my goals and progress. I will never ask more of you than I am willing to give of myself."

Finally, I assured them I would have their backs, and I felt confident they would have mine.

After this first meeting, I administered practices for building a community and a responsible, productive culture. Some of the salient practices were as follows:

The Basics

Model Behaviors

I instituted weekly meetings and often used them to model strong communication behaviors. For example, I would sit in the middle of the boardroom table and ask open-ended questions, indicating my desire to hear their ideas and letting them know I wanted them to talk and listen to each other. I also allowed myself to stay open to constructive criticism, asking questions like, "What needs to be changed?" and I encouraged honesty.

Demonstrate Personal Interest

I generally held one-on-one meetings with each team member in addition to weekly team meetings. We met every three to four weeks to discuss achievements and problems so we could immediately respond to challenges and acknowledge wins, no matter how big or small. These meetings served several purposes—problems could be addressed and managed before yearly performance reviews, and noting "wins" empowered direct reports and executives alike. Furthermore, these meetings served to create personal bonds that helped to build trust and empathy.

I followed the principle of "managing by walking around"[1] to help build community. When I entered a room, I did my best to acknowledge whoever was in the office. I had an authentic and genuine interest in how people were feeling personally, and I spoke to employees at all levels. My hope was that everyone would realize they were seen holistically, not just as workers.

We recognized personal events such as births, deaths, and personal accomplishments in our employees' families. We spend more time with our coworkers than with our families. Knowing what employees enjoy in their time off is therefore equally important as knowing how they perform in the office.

Provide Opportunities for Connection

I required regular team meetings to augment relationships and exchange information. Team members would decide when to meet and what to discuss, and our director of client services helped to keep these meetings on track. We also planned an annual office activity to relieve stress and enjoy each other's company. I believed this was important, as chronic stress in the workplace can overwhelm our ability to take in new information and generate new ideas. A fun activity can relieve stress, renew positive feelings, and strengthen our ability to learn.[2]

Managing and Preventing Conflict

Often our meeting agendas included time for debates and airing of disagreements. These potentially emotionally charged conversations were preceded by mindful discussions on how to debate and listen respectfully.

I taught my team how to deliver criticism so the person receiving it hears an additional idea, not an attack. I often suggested phrasing their criticism by saying, "When you said _____, I thought you hadn't thought about _____."

When I received criticism, I nodded in acknowledgment and paraphrased what I heard, letting that person know I was listening and that I cared about what they were saying.

Other Principles for Building a Strong Culture

Holding employees accountable is a test of trust. If they are surprised by the criteria being used to evaluate their performance, trust in management erodes. I advise employees about my expectation that they demonstrate two important principles:

Integrity: If mistakes are made or something goes wrong for a client, do not make excuses. It is our problem, and the client looks to us to fix it. We have tools the client does not have and can build trust if we prove we are responsible.

Honesty: If you drop a ball or worse, lose an account, do not be afraid to tell me. Inevitably we will lose some business. Our responsibility is to learn from the loss. What happened? What could have been improved? What lessons do we take to our other clients?

Winning Back Our Client

Immediately after hearing about the long-term client's RFP, our team huddled to share information and strategize. A suggestion was made to create a video for our client instead of sending a three-page executive summary reciting how we have provided excellent service. The video would introduce our client to the people who help them in the background, show how they have served them, and explain what they could expect from them in the future. The video might capture someone walking down the hall, waving hello, and stopping to chat. This approach offered many opportunities to creatively illustrate our value proposition and remind the client that we are person-focused.

When this project was announced, team members responded instantly. One team member offered to film the video. Another said, "I don't have anything going on tonight. I'll stay late." Others joined in, volunteering to take on extra work and work longer hours. Even an employee from a different team offered to help with the extensive printing needs. It was a demanding project, and most lost a little sleep over the pressure and longer hours, but the impulse to help each other and win back our client created a momentum that overshadowed the sacrifices.

In addition to creating the video, I urged our team to overprepare for their presentation. Again, the team exceeded expectations and practiced their presentation more than ten times. They critiqued each other respectfully, as they had learned in our debates. They did not stop until they felt confident they were ready.

Our client understood the subtext of our presentation upon viewing our project. The video reminded them of the services we had delivered, but they also noticed our caring culture. The video portrayed an energetic team who seemed connected to each other and devoted to building value together. The subtext was: if this is how the employees work within their company, then clients will certainly receive the same kind of care and resourcefulness.

After the contract was signed, our team celebrated. We lunched at a favorite restaurant and tipped our glasses to our success. However, we also reviewed our experience. We recounted what went well and what we could learn from our mistakes. Foremost in everyone's mind was how they had picked each other up during the process, regenerating energy, and hope. There had been moments of frustration and insecurity, but they were diminished when someone extended help and encouragement.

Reflecting on My Leadership Journey

I had not expected to become the president of our business unit and I was surprised when I was asked if I had an interest in the position. Initially, I declined and felt great relief in doing so. I had been very successful in sales, and I did not feel confident in my leadership skills. However, I was elected to our company's women's executive board. This group was unlike any other I had experienced. Board members were elevating and championing each other, and there was a human connection that was authentic and empowering. The support and development I received as part of this group enabled me to believe I had the capacity to be an effective leader. Our work on how to approach leadership, both cognitively and emotionally, built my leadership skills as well as my confidence.

Later, when I became unit president, I decided to look at this opportunity as a chance to build an internal business community similar to the women's executive board. In addition to instilling accountability, transparency, and integrity as driving principles of our community, I aimed to develop a culture that included caring and nurturing. I wanted to encourage a sense of self-confidence and self-worth such that employees would feel confident in accepting the opportunities and challenges presented to them.

Our success in winning back our long-term client not only demonstrated our achievement in creating a caring and responsible culture but this culture's ability to lend itself to business survival. I am grateful to the women's executive board for teaching me their unconventional leadership methods. As I reflect on their work, I see an inspiring contrast between how women have been traditionally viewed and how many women are presenting themselves today. Often in business, women are merely springboards for men to take center stage. But the women on our executive board were themselves accomplished and dared to share wisdom and raised their hands often to take center stage. They empowered me and other women to lead, and to lead differently.

While I appreciate what the women's executive board did for me, I am also thankful for the employees I led. They courageously adapted to changes in our daily practices, and they were prepared to take risks. I am forever proud of the work I have done but equally proud of the employees in our business unit who worked beside me. Together, we created great collaborations.

Strengthening the Heart
of Human Connection

By Lisa Lochner

ACROSS AMERICA, SMALL-TOWN HOSPITALS are the heartbeat of their communities, the main resource for everything from a sprained ankle to a psychotic episode. The staff become the confidantes and supportive shoulders when people are going through a crisis, sitting by the bedside of an ill loved one, or finding themselves on the receiving end of a terrifying diagnosis. The providers, nurses, and entire team are a sort of extended family who are interwoven into every aspect of the town's fabric. They're often people we grew up with, friends from high school, or the neighbor you pass on your way to work.

When something as life-upending as COVID strikes, it has a massive ripple effect for everyone in the hospital and in the community. When the pandemic started, I was a leader in our local critical access hospital in an area with a population just under ten thousand. I grew up in that town and knew many of the people who came through the doors of the hospital. So when I was serving as the COVID incident commander, I had a personal and professional investment in making sure my staff was as well cared for as our patients.

I had been hired as the Human Resources Manager many years before and worked my way up through the ranks until I was promoted to president during the second year of the COVID pandemic. By that time, the staff was exhausted, both mentally and physically, by the continual drain on resources, energy, and optimism. Many of my team members lived in the communities we served and watched people they knew die before their eyes. Every day was heart-wrenching, and it was one of the most difficult situations anyone in the medical field had ever endured.

A couple of years earlier, I had considered leaving the hospital and taking a position at another facility, not only to have a different experience but to distance myself emotionally. It's incredibly difficult to work in a place where people you know are experiencing joy and tragedy. But then I came back to my *why* for working there. The thing that made it so difficult was the same reason I wanted to be there—because every patient was part of my community. And I wanted to be sure that my neighbors were being cared for in the best possible way.

The first COVID patient who came into our hospital was someone I knew. So many people in our community got deathly ill or died. Yet none of us could talk about the trauma of enduring such painful events because of HIPAA confidentiality rules. The masks we wore and the plastic dividing the sections of the hospital created physical walls. But I could see so many more emotional walls going up as the necessary isolation of the pandemic broke down relationships and communication. Even as staff members worked together to save lives, I could see fragments in their relationships with each other. People were becoming increasingly isolated and siloed, both at home and at work.

All of this took a massive emotional toll on our team members. People who work in a hospital feel a personal mission to save lives, and when the virus began taking lives despite our most valiant efforts, it was devastating. What some of our staff endured during a single shift made me wonder where they found the strength to come back the next day. The "heroes work here" phrase was evident in every corner of our hospital, but like other frontline workers during COVID, we were cracking under the chaos and pressure. Our community was hurting, both within and outside the hospital walls. We needed to rebuild the relationships and trust among our team. We needed to create a space that felt safe and supportive, even with social distancing and hazmat precautions. We needed to let our staff know that we understood the physical and emotional burden this cataclysmic event had placed on them.

Even though I knew the pandemic would eventually become more manageable, it was clear my team of more than four hundred people was emotionally depleted and mentally defeated. When I was interviewing for the president's position, I came across a quote from Sarah Jane-Redmond that said, "A successful team beats with one heart." That quote became the foundation of my One Heart, One Team program—designed to help facilitate connections, conversations, and support.

During COVID, information and protocols were changing rapidly, sometimes hour by hour. This meant it was critical that we had a way to communicate these changing directions with transparency and clarity. I started with a daily check-in with my senior leadership team and other key team members. I met with department managers regularly to keep them aware of changes and priorities. I spoke to team members to communicate the mission of the new program. I shadowed someone from each department so I could deepen my knowledge of their specialty and increase my connection with every part of the hospital. I stepped outside of my normal work hours and began intentional rounding with all the shifts on a regular basis. I wanted the people who worked nights and weekends to know that we cared about their needs just as much as we did everyone else's.

There were other small things that kept the message going. All supervisors received "One Heart, One Team" T-shirts. They gave every member of their team "One Heart, One Team" pens and notepads. We used the phrase in all of our messaging. We showed it in actions that promoted their financial, health, and mental well-being, such as discounts in the cafeteria, a massage chair that rotated between departments, and a stocked team member snack cart.

The National Institutes of Health has done numerous studies on mental health and well-being in the workplace. There are so many correlations between how employees feel, how they perform, and the environment they create based on how they are feeling.[3] Well-being doesn't have to be a spa appointment—it can be something as simple as taking a moment to ask a team member if there is anything they need.

I wanted to give my leadership team a way to vent, so I held team-building sessions at my home. We didn't have an agenda for the meeting; instead, I said, "We're going to just talk about what's on your mind, what's getting in your way, and how you are feeling. Let's get it all out on the table." I had no idea how it would go—whether I would get crickets or rants in return.

We sat around my dining room table, learning from one another, listening with compassion, and seeing each person with open eyes. I admit there were moments when it was difficult for me to sit there and simply listen to what was working and what wasn't. My staff told me they were exhausted, understaffed, overworked. We discussed ways to alleviate those burdens. At the end of the conversation, many of them asked if we could do it again.

This session led the leadership team to take the same approach with our entire group of team leaders. We followed the same intent of letting them vent during the regularly scheduled two-hour monthly meetings. The conversations were vulnerable and heartfelt, with many openly sharing their feelings. To give shyer people an opportunity to speak up, we offered some small-group offshoot meetings. With the leadership team, we increased our level of accountability to each other and the larger team by adding "I will" to our commitment to each other instead of "I will strive," which we hoped would create a cascade of workplace commitments for the year and accountability across the organization.

With patriarchal leadership, care ethics take second place to virtue theory, which focuses on the individual.[4] With matriarchal leadership, care and relationships come first. The entire environment is designed around consideration. And in a hospital setting, what better place to begin than with care?

This is how a leader transforms rhetoric into a promise. It's how you tell your team, "I see you. I value you. I appreciate you." It's how you transform a team culture, and by extension, the community around that team.

In our workplace today, spirits have been revived, but more importantly, we are seeing the impact of One Heart, One Team in the metrics. For the first time in its sixty-year history, our hospital recently received a five-star quality award. The company that oversees our patient satisfaction results gave us an Outstanding Culture Award—again a first in our history to receive. Our patient satisfaction scores now regularly exceed our targets, and we have been able to increase our annual budget. The momentum from our One Heart, One Team effort has compounded in value month over month, year over year. This tiny hospital built in the sixties now has received over $100 million in improvements instituted or on the way, from a new addition to our imaging center to an expansion of the emergency room. The system is investing in us because they have confidence in the team, while the leadership has confidence in the caregiving team, and the patients have confidence in their caregivers.

Our team is there for our community—our neighbors—whether that's to repair a hernia or help them apply for other needed resources.

We have seen the mental health toll of the pandemic and have strengthened our mental health resources. We see the needs of the people around us and are doing our best to answer them every day. For myself, I have made sure my availability extends beyond the work walls. I want the community to know that if they have a question about their bill or a concern about an upcoming surgery, I am there as their neighbor and friend.

As with anything, the One Heart, One Team vibe ebbs and flows. We have good days and bad, but throughout it all, we continue to communicate by leaving the door open and inviting conversations. We hang the banners in the hallways, but we reinforce that messaging with continual action.

The other day, a shift report came across my desk. One of the team members had had an especially difficult and draining night. Just below that, a second team member had written, "One Heart, One Team" and added a smiley face. We care—and we tell each other often.

You Matter

By Anne Richards

GOODWILL OF GREATER CLEVELAND and East Central Ohio first opened its doors 105 years ago in an old warehouse in Cleveland. I am the first woman and first known member of the LGBTQ+ community to be the President and CEO. For over six years, I have held this position. I reached this level in my career at a turbulent time in the business and under difficult circumstances. It was November 2016. Sales were poor, morale was low, and talent was weak when the then-current CEO summoned me to his hospital room. He told me he had less than six weeks to live and our $28 million agency was now mine to run. To make matters worse, two weeks before the CEO passed away, a devastating fire destroyed all the donations we had saved to get us through the winter.

Sadly, the CEO passed away just three weeks after the day I met with him in his hospital room. During those three short weeks, he and I spent several hours together—the teacher and the pupil. I absorbed everything I could from him, wanting to extract as much operational knowledge as possible. In addition to the operational knowledge, he also wanted to provide guidance on the people side of the business. He gave me one especially important caution. He said, "As the CEO, people won't come to you like they do now. No one will want to talk to you. It is very lonely at top."

I wondered if he was right. In my then-twenty years of human resource experience, people frequently came to me. My door always revolved with employees coming in and going out. I was known for making time for others and doing my best to demonstrate how much I cared. My strength had always been my ability to connect with others, and I'd planned to rely on it heavily. Sitting beside the CEO's hospital bed, I felt anything but lonely. But would that change?

On a cold December day, I found myself dealing with a fire, the CEO's impending death, slumping sales, significant talent gaps in key positions, and a board that not only adored the previous CEO but had no desire to move on from him. Although the operational knowledge I received from the previous CEO was invaluable, I felt the people side of the business was my strength—and that strength would pull us through. But was I right?

After five years as the Vice President of Human Resources, I understood our company's culture and knew we needed to fix it. Employees didn't feel valued, engagement was low, accountability was lacking, and results were poor. We hadn't captured employees' hearts and sometimes not even their heads or their hands. We needed to create a culture where employees wanted to be at work and they knew they mattered.

My first order of business was to find the right leaders and make sure they were placed appropriately. When I became the CEO, we had some leaders who lacked approachability, integrity, and even kindness. One of the first steps I took was to clearly explain my expectations of leaders to the management staff. I called a meeting, stood in front of them, and said, "Leaders must be approachable, empathetic, available, and honest. If we focus on demonstrating good leadership traits, we won't have to worry about results—they will follow." And I immediately recognized the need to fix my own house first.

Two members of the senior leadership team were not approachable, lacked empathy, and were detrimental to the culture I wanted to create. One of them did display above average results, but that didn't matter to me. I was determined to achieve my most important objective. Employees were not going to be treated in a way that made them feel like just warm bodies to management. Within sixty days of my becoming the CEO, one of those leaders was gone, and the other followed approximately one hundred days later. I was not unhappy about this since their values obviously did not align with the culture we were working to develop.

While I was dealing with the issues with the senior leadership team, we had sessions with other members of management about expected behaviors. Leaders had to exemplify respect, honesty, transparency, approachability, availability, and kindness. No longer were people going to hold leadership positions if they obtained good results through bullying, intimidation, and manipulation. Instead, expectations were tied to our organization's values, and our organization's values were tied to employee performance evaluations, which ultimately tied to compensation. If leaders could not live up to our expected behaviors and values, they either left on their own or were asked to leave—regardless of the results they produced.

Within six months of my becoming the CEO, we gave our culture a name, formally calling it, "You Matter." This was long before the "You Matter" theme became mainstream like it is today. We purchased shirts and wristbands for all our employees with this verbiage. We held day-long training sessions to educate employees on what "You Matter" meant and the connected behaviors we expected. I recorded videos explaining the culture and what we were trying to create. We developed a committee of employees from all levels of the organization to help with culture changes and shifts. Surveys were used to create a baseline of how employees viewed the environment.

During my first year as the CEO, several members of the management team were replaced, but the results were getting better, and we were on our way. However, there is never a period at the end of the cultural sentence. It is always changing, evolving, renewing. Leaders need to keep an eye on the workplace atmosphere, pay attention to it, and measure it to ensure it doesn't head down the wrong path. At our organization, we do this through pulse surveys, stay interviews, exit interviews, town halls with all employees, and other avenues for employees to connect directly with me and with members of management.

Fast-forward to today, and where are we? Six years ago, we were a $28 million organization, $11 million in debt, with $4 million in the bank. Today, we are a $44 million organization, debt-free, with close to $14 million in the bank. We've completely flipped the balance sheet, even through the COVID years. We are not without challenges and issues, but the culture is much healthier than it was six years ago. Employees feel more heard and respected. Relationships are deeper and more connected. One key indicator proves our model through the longevity milestones employees are reaching: instead of just having a few employees celebrating their five- and ten-year anniversaries, now we have many. If you ask employees today how they feel about the organization, I believe most who were here prior to me becoming CEO would characterize the culture now as kinder, gentler, and more welcoming. Turnover in the salaried staff dropped from over 30 percent to under 5 percent in the first two years of "You Matter." Turnover in the salaried staff continues at those levels. Relationships between management and employees and between employees and the CEO are stronger and deeper.

I sometimes think about the caution the previous CEO gave me: "As the CEO, people won't come to you like they do now. No one will want to talk to you. It is very lonely at the top."

I am happy to say that has not been my experience. My phone rings and beeps constantly. My office door revolves with employees going in and out. I have just as many people visiting me today in my role as CEO as used to visit me when I was vice president of human resources. My leadership style is about being approachable and available to everyone. My door is always open. Everyone knows it, and I don't even have a gatekeeper. Any employee can stop by anytime. The culture is different than it was six years ago. The leaders are different. Morale is better. And the results speak for themselves.

Three Pillars for Successfully Transforming Corporate Culture

By Lorri Slesh

I WAS ON A ropes course, of all places, when I saw firsthand how to take a negative environment and transform it into a positive, supportive culture filled with enthusiastic team members. Fresh out of college, I led an adventure course for a group of teenagers who were struggling with trust, confidence, and self-esteem. They were frustrated with their parents and teachers because they felt like no one was listening to them or seeing their true selves. When they first arrived, most of these teens were skeptical and unenthusiastic. Sounds like the employees at your typical company, right?

If you sit employees down and ask them what bothers them most about their current company culture, they'll talk about feeling siloed or being seen as a cog in the machine rather than as an individual. These emotions have a direct correlation to a reduction in not only employee efficiency[5] but also morale.[6]

A couple years ago, I was called in to help a start-up about to burst at the seams. They had plenty of work and a massive target to meet and were taking on employees as quickly as they could. Like many start-ups, they had no formal onboarding process or human resources department, which made for chaotic hiring. I stepped into the role of Human Resources Manager, but my job was about much more than making sure everyone signed up for the company insurance policy. I was there to build an environment of trust, support, and inspiration.

Of our several dozen new employees spread across the country, most of them worked from home. The challenge was building a community from afar. It's impossible to do that in a video conference, so I needed to be ingenious in building the company culture. I decided to focus on KPIs—not key performance indicators but rather key *people* indicators. I was more interested in whether the employees felt valued and connected than whether we met a particular sales goal. I knew if the team members were invested in the company and each other, the start-up's culture would become a positive and powerful force for overall company success.

The First Pillar: Trust

Trust is essential in every workplace.[7] It allows staff to feel safe, not only so they can do their jobs but also so they can ask questions and grow to the next level. That trust is built from the relationships formed at work. People get to know each other and feel some level of connection, which in turn cultivates trust. Women in particular build trust in the workplace by sharing information about themselves.[8] There's a delicate balance, however, between sharing a personal history of trauma, for instance, and sharing something less vulnerable. Sitting in the human resources seat is, by nature, a challenging balance when it comes to building the trust of employees and leadership. I had seen the same situation on the ropes course.

Many of the troubled teens I'd worked with had lived difficult lives filled with the growing pains of being a teenager and dealing with dysfunctional family dynamics. None of them were going to open up about the details with people they didn't know. But they would talk about the challenges of the course, the beauty of nature around them, and their fears of crossing a swaying bridge. Instant friendships were formed among people who said, "You've got this," to each other.

I wanted to communicate the same thing to our distanced and disparate workforce. Over the first few months, I sat down with each team member to have a casual conversation about their role, their thoughts about the workplace, and their hobbies outside of work. I didn't assign behavioral assessments because I didn't want to make this seem like a quiz, nor did I want people to start engaging in prescribed behavioral ways because they had been labeled with a specific set of strengths, tendencies, and weaknesses.

Instead, the intentionality behind these conversations created a way to let the employees know the company was interested in them as human beings. I've learned culture-building should be seen through the lens of employee engagement and interaction. If employees don't care (or feel like leadership doesn't care), no amount of donuts on Fridays will improve that situation.

Back when I was leading the adventure courses, I read a book called *Tribes* by Jeanne Gibbs. She talked about the importance of inclusion, influence, and affection in building a positive school environment. When we are young, that often happens via extracurricular activities, from sports to campus clubs. Studies have shown that these extracurricular activities are vital in student retention and satisfaction.[9] Why do we not think to use the same approach in the workforce?

I compiled the team members' interests into categories ranging from working out to playing board games and used those to build several affinity groups: Actives, Gamers, Do-Gooders, Media Consumers, and Creatives. Since this was a biotechnology start-up, I called the affinity groups Biomes. The leadership team okayed a modest budget for each team, and I appointed volunteer coordinators for each group.

We brainstormed fun events that fit each group's personality and interests. There were photo scavenger hunts, fitness challenges, book clubs, and costume contests. Some groups tried glass blowing while others immersed themselves in the Van Gogh art experience.

We used photos of the Biomes in action on our internal and external social media posts as well as on our website's career page. We invited our summer interns to participate in the Mario Kart racing and yard games. All of this sent the message that our company cared about their employees as people, not simply as workers.

The end result was easy to see. Team members felt seen because we answered the call for their individual interests. They felt safe because they were in groups of people like themselves. They felt inspired because they knew this was much more than an ordinary job. All of these feelings built a strong foundation of trust throughout the company.

The Second Pillar: Support

Next, we organized an in-person summit for all team members. Our Biomes groups had begun the necessary relationship-building work, and now we were going to put those principles into place in person. We planned a wide variety of activities for the summit, from an evening at Topgolf to a pottery class, all designed to meet the interests of each of the Biomes.

Simple things, like allowing each team member to order their own lunch from a selection of restaurants we had engaged to deliver, sent subtle messages that we weren't trying to fit everyone into a rubber-chicken, conference meal box. People were ecstatic that they could have autonomy over their own meals. It was less of a logistical headache than I expected, and it resulted in saving the company a lot of money because people finished their meals and there was little to no waste.

We also concentrated on employee recognition by handing out awards for service and outstanding performance. Even after the summit ended, we made kudos a regular part of the culture. Leadership was empowered to hand out spot bonuses to individuals who were innovative, who collaborated well, or who met tough deadlines. We also announced a referral bonus program to help attract and retain talent.

Through these efforts, team members realized that we not only saw and appreciated their hard work but that we were there to support them as they grew. The relational culture theory originally posited by Jean Baker Miller[10] is based on the thinking that relationships with peers are catalysts for growth. Essentially, people do not grow alone, and by building the Biomes and showing regular support, we were able to create a culture of connectivity that bolstered everyone.

The Third Pillar: Inspiration

This biotech start-up was on the cutting edge of many technological advances. They wanted to continue to encourage innovative thinking by building a hip, inspiring environment. We needed to create an internal corporate structure to foster the same inspirational thinking. We had already established trust and support—the ropes holding up the bridge of innovation that would get the company to its next destination.

I set up a variety of task forces and populated them with team members to encourage continued engagement. Instead of doing annual reviews, I instituted a quarterly review process. With today's workforce, if you wait a year, your retention, engagement, and job satisfaction are going to suffer.

We established cascading goals for each department and each employee. I then worked with the finance department to create a professional development policy where employees could submit proposals for courses and certifications that would enhance their skill sets in their current role or a potential new role within the company. I also applied for grants that would pay for additional employee professional development.

On the ropes course, I distinctly remember seeing the fear on some of the teenagers' faces before they crossed the bridge. But because we had done the work on the ground of building relationships, their peers were there to encourage them as they took that first step. We can follow the same successful methodology with a start-up—there's a lot of fear and chaos in meeting goals and securing funding. But if you do the work with your team to build a functional, supportive, communicative group, the start-up will have a strong, enthusiastic foundation.

A couple months after the summit, I looked at my key people indicators. In HR, those numbers are reflected in hiring, retention, and turnover. As a culmination of employee satisfaction, I enrolled the company in a "top places to work" survey. We had a 98 percent participation rate and won the company's first Top Places to Work Award. In terms of key performance indicators, the start-up won numerous industry awards and closed a $33 million Series B funding round. It was, in all respects, a success. But this wasn't what really told me my efforts had paid off.

A comment in the Zoom channel group chat said, "When's the next mystery ingredient cook-off? Can't wait to do that again!" Thanks to the foundation of our three pillars, this comment confirmed that we had successfully transformed our corporate culture.

Building High-Functioning Cultures of Inclusion and Trust

By Dr. Rachel-Yvonne Talton

The Genesis of Synergy

When I was six years old, I watched the movie *Sybil*, about a young girl who had twenty-seven distinct personalities. I was spellbound and wanted to leap into the television to help her. From that moment, I've been on a mission to help people build emotional connections with themselves, with their loved ones and peers, and with the brands and causes they support. Particularly as a Black woman, I have ignited during this journey a deep-seated passion and expertise for exploring the emotional nexus between trust and inclusivity. After all, in the business world, trust is one of your most significant assets.[11]

I graduated at the top 10 percent of my class with an executive MBA from Cleveland State University with a concentration in finance while I worked for National City Bank. I then went to Case Western Reserve University to pursue a PhD in management. Since there had been so much turmoil in the banking industry from 2006 to 2008, I developed my research area on understanding how to create and sustain a beloved organization. My studies taught me that organizations cannot create love, though they can build, maintain, and repair trust in order to create the perception of satisfaction and loyalty.[12] That was when I left the bank and founded Synergy International Limited, Inc. My mission is to help organizations leverage the intersection of inclusion and trust with all their stakeholders.

Trust is a prerequisite for every transaction, and I would submit that inclusion is equally important. Inclusive organizations experience higher engagement, better retention rates, greater profitability,[13] and an improved ability to attract the best and brightest employees. In fact, 78 percent of people believe that DEIB (diversity, equity, inclusion, and belonging) offers a competitive advantage. Eighty percent of surveyed job seekers say that a commitment to DEIB is vital when choosing between employers.[14]

Since founding Synergy International Limited, Inc, my vision has been driven by two guiding principles: First, helping organizations and their leaders become more inclusive across the thirty-six dimensions of diversity. Second, helping them build and maintain the trust of their stakeholders. The sustainability of *our* brand is embedded within this commitment.

Defining Organizational Culture

There have been numerous definitions of *culture*, but through my research, I've found there is one definition that stands out. According to SHRM (the Society for Human Resource Management),[15] "an organization's culture consists of shared beliefs and values established by leaders and then communicated and reinforced through various methods, ultimately shaping employee perceptions, behaviors, and understanding. Organizational culture sets the context for everything an enterprise does. Because industries vary significantly, there is not a one-size-fits-all culture template that meets the needs of all organizations."

In a healthy organizational culture, trust is critical. How leaders and brands build trust, maintain it, and repair it when it has been violated is more important today than ever before.[16] Leaders shape and reinforce cultures by what they pay attention to and how they behave. For the trustworthiness of a leader to be valued, it must embody the following three dimensions:

- Competency: Do you have the skills and experience?
- Integrity: Are values shared and are you transparent?
- Benevolence: Do you have another's best interest at heart?

Additionally, inclusion is critical to building a healthy organizational culture and drives financial returns.[17]

Creating Trusted and Inclusive Leaders in the Workplace Culture

I've been fortunate to be engaged in and witness the groundbreaking success of organizations investing in their culture. In contrast, I have also seen organizations that lack the will to build and maintain trust and inclusion in the work environment. They fail to capture the benefits in their bottom-line results.

Organizations like Amazon, AWS, Pinterest, Toyota, Mars, Incorporated, rag + bone, Miller's Ale House, John Hardy, and many others call upon Synergy when there is a lack of cohesion or trust and/or their organization requires a more strategic approach to corporate inclusion. An excellent example occurred with one of our global clients.

I'll call the executive of this global technology company Vanessa. She has a team of eleven direct reports with varying tenure in the organization, diverse educations, and differing levels of experience in the tech space. She had been in the role for a little over two years when her responsibility was set to increase. She understood that if she did not get her team aligned, she would not meet her potential for success in her expanded role. She called, and we spoke about the responsibilities of her team, her understanding of their opportunities and challenges, and what she would like to accomplish in our time together. I told her our engagement would be for a minimum of one year and we would start with a two-day retreat.

Prior to the retreat, my team and I conducted one-on-one interviews with each of Vanessa's direct reports, creating a deeper qualitative understanding of their needs, opportunities, and challenges. We also implemented two assessments. First, the Hogan Leadership Assessment,[18] which measures reputation, meaning what everyone else thinks of you, and is based on overt behaviors and social skills. Reputation is the person other people think you are, and success in the workplace is dependent on reputation. We also conducted the 360 Inclusive Leadership Compass (360 ILC),[19] which is a multirater feedback tool that measures inclusive leadership effectiveness and identifies everyday actions to support behavioral change.

To ensure authentic and genuine discussions, our consulting projects begin with communicating the ground rules so we can accomplish our objectives during this discovery phase. Members are asked to honor confidentiality, embrace their own vulnerability, listen to understand, respect all opinions, and be present and focused on the task at hand. We open every consulting session with a series of thought-provoking questions related to the client's specific needs.

We designed the two-day retreat based on our model of building trust—which requires time for reflection and building community. With Vanessa's company, we conducted an exercise called "The Story of You," which calls for each participant to take a self-discovery journey to what makes you, well, *you*.

These five levels consist of:

- Peak Experiences: Moments that shaped you for the better. Big wins.
- Valley Experiences: Moments of sadness, disappointment, or painful transition.
- Major Milestones: Any pivotal decisions or milestones that dramatically impacted your course.
- Defining Milestones: Key defining moments that shaped your life's work.
- And finally, participants are asked to author their future: Identify three powerful things you can control that will design the future you deserve.

During the session, the group is engaged and surprisingly transparent, and participants leave with a new level of hope that they can work more effectively.[20] They have a foundation for building more cohesion in their work relationships. There is always transformation that happens in a room when we create psychological safety and people allow themselves to be vulnerable.[21]

The Hogan Assessment provides a wonderful opportunity for people to uncover their strengths, and importantly, their *overused* strengths (which are often derailers). In the context of work culture, overused strengths can become derailers when they're deployed to such an extent that they impede progress, disrupt team dynamics, or foster negative outcomes. For example, an individual with strong attention to detail might derail a project if their perfectionism causes them to focus excessively on minutiae, thereby slowing down the project progress. The concept is supported by research that has found that leaders who overuse particular strengths, such as focusing too much on results at the expense of team cohesion, could end up eroding trust, limiting efficacy, and disrupting innovation.[22] We then discuss how they might leverage strengths and mitigate weaknesses. The assessment also uncovers the values of the individuals on the team so people can connect around those values.[23]

The ILC 360 tool allows leaders to understand if they are being experienced as inclusive and where they have opportunities to grow. Some of them find that coaching is a deficit and they need to raise team engagement. Some find that to better unlock the full potential of their teams, inclusion must run through the core of the organization. Business systems should align to reinforce behaviors to sustain cultural shifts. In all cases, participants learn more about themselves and their peers.

Working with Vanessa's organization, we finally developed a Flourish 100-Day Leadership Development Plan. Participants chose three elements they would work on with their accountability partner over the next one hundred days.[24]

This outline represents the starting points of work we do with teams. We begin with an in-person gathering (when possible) and a minimum of four four-hour sessions with the group throughout the year. We worked with Vanessa's team quarterly and had an additional one-on-one session with each of the leaders. Two of these leaders asked us to come in and do a similar in-person session with their teams. At the end of the year, there were a number of breakthroughs, new innovations, more team cohesion, improved relationships, and cocreation of projects and programs, and Vanessa received her highest performance review ever.

In organizations where culture is not prioritized, leadership can get so focused on task delivery that the priorities and needs of their most valuable asset, their people, fade away. One of the greatest professional lessons I've learned is that you must define, meet, and seek to exceed the needs of people in your organization. And then one must sustain the collective—a community of clients and customers, stakeholders, employees, and prospective customers—in order to achieve success.

Sustaining a Culture of High Trust and High Inclusion

As workforces continue to evolve, the ability of an organization to adapt and respond to change will remain its most valuable skill and ability. To promote the trust of talent, it is necessary to have an inclusive mindset. This implies that the leader recognizes the gift of having diverse voices in their team. Inclusion improves product creation, customer service, risk assessment, and innovation. Embracing vigorously discussed ideas in a comfortable manner allows for better business outcomes in addition to each person's growth. This enhances trust, as each team member observes how they are valued for what they bring to the organization.

Neuroscience has shown that when someone trusts, a jolt of oxytocin surges through the brain and triggers reciprocation.[25] This creates a trust-building cycle, which leads to more learning, openness to alternative perspectives, reciprocity in communication and collaboration, and increased psychological safety. People perform better when they trust the people they work with, when relationships are deeply valued, and when leaders are credible, competent, communicative, and honest. They believe they are treated with respect as people and professionals and the workplace is fundamentally fair.

In order to sustain a high level of trust and inclusion on your team, here are a few tools we have found helpful:

- Keep roles and responsibilities clear. One of the best ways to get people to trust each other is to make clear what every member of the team is responsible for. This also means having a clear understanding of their colleagues' roles and responsibilities.
- Open your network and make introductions to people who can help an employee progress in their career.
- Praise (with specificity and regularity) team members' work to executives in the organization.
- Beware of unconscious biases and ask yourself what assumptions you may be making about a person or situation.
- Ask yourself how an employee or group of employees is experiencing a situation differently than you might experience it.
- Find out what your team needs in order to do their best work and discover how they best communicate.
- Offer networking opportunities for team members to share their capabilities.
- Encourage and role model transparency. Leaders can emphasize the importance of being open and honest by inviting team members to regularly share their challenges as well as their successes—during meetings or in an internal forum. Open them up for discussion.
- Empower your team to be self-organized. People trust each other more when they make decisions together.
- Be vulnerable, genuinely solicit the input of others, and always admit, even advertise, what you don't know.
- Assess the levels of belonging in individuals in your organization. Four of the key elements of belonging are connection, participation, identification, and congruence.

- Create opportunities for cocreation and innovation. To build trust, people must problem-solve together and rely on each other. A great opportunity for teams to build these skills is tackling tasks outside of their day-to-day.

I always say that we don't succeed unless our clients do. That's why I call this work my GodJob (I really must trademark that)! Because when I am able to build teams that can innovate, communicate, and collaborate effectively and inclusively, I am able to achieve the purpose for which I was born.

MUTUALITY LESSONS LEARNED

How did leaders in this chapter foster mutuality?

When **Karen Grasso** became president of her company, she knew she needed to transform the existing uncaring and disparate culture into a culture of community. Some of the most salient tactics she used include setting an example of transparency and accountability, demonstrating interest and care for employees' personal lives, and teaching her team specific methods for maintaining harmony while debating potentially divisive issues and behaviors.

These techniques cultivated a synergistic and collaborative team and resulted in creative solutions that helped the company overcome powerful competition.

As president of a hospital during the chaos of the COVID pandemic, **Lisa Lochner** observed her staff struggling to meet the demands of constant operational disruptions while trying to manage emotions stirred by witnessing an inconceivable increase in suffering and death.

Lisa responded by fostering mutuality to mitigate the fragmentation of relationships, roles, and responsibilities. She accomplished this through effective messaging and increasing opportunities to interface with and learn from employees. She made the message "One Heart, One Team" visible throughout the facility and included it in communications. Meetings were intentionally designed to enhance employees' well-being. For example, Lisa experimented with a meeting where the only agenda was to allow personal discussions of frustrations and discontent. She held this meeting in her home, reinforcing the idea that Lisa cared about her employees personally. The meeting produced suggestions for reducing employees' burdens and increased the sense of a caring, responsible community. This type of meeting was repeated with more team leaders, furthering the sense of mutuality.

Lisa's focus on mutuality resulted in superior ratings and appreciable increases in financial investments from the larger hospital system.

Before becoming CEO of Goodwill of Greater Cleveland and East Central Ohio, **Anne Richards** knew that the organization's culture was stifling productivity. Sales were poor and morale was low. Conversations with her predecessor revealed a disconnect between management and employees.

Anne developed a program exemplifying mutuality to change the culture. She captured the notion of mutuality in a simple message: "You Matter." She spotlighted and disseminated this message throughout the organization through a day-long training session, multilevel committees that reinforced the message, interviews with employees, and town halls. Additionally, she encouraged employees to come into her office, unlike her predecessor.

Results indicate that mutuality was a factor contributing to success. Sales increased dramatically, and cash-on-hand grew from $4 million to $14 million, even through COVID. Furthermore, turnover dropped significantly among salaried staff. Anne accomplished all of this in six short years, despite the ineffective culture she inherited and a fire that destroyed inventory weeks before she took office.

Lorri Slesh was hired as the human resources manager for a start-up company and was tasked with building an environment of trust, support, and inspiration for remote employees. Her methods and aims for accomplishing this reflect mutuality. She conducted interviews with employees to learn about their beliefs about the workplace and their personal hobbies. Using this information, she created Biomes, or social affinity groups, and importantly, she obtained funding for event planning for each Biome. The activities and events helped employees create trusting bonds. The company enhanced these connections by creating an in-person summit where all Biomes met and participated in activities. The company also gave the Biomes visibility by posting pictures of the events on social media and websites. These practices encouraged mutuality by creating opportunities to create relationships that increased sharing of information.

Lorri also encouraged mutuality between employees and the company by working with the finance department and applying for grants to fund professional development. Together these strategies resulted in several awards and a $33 million grant.

When **Rachel Talton** works with organizations to transform cultures to be more inclusive and trusting, she utilizes methods centering on self-reflection and interpersonal discussions. These methods mirror mutuality. She interviews employees, seeking their input, and she conducts assessments and exercises such as "The Story of You" to stimulate introspection. She also sets clear ground rules for discussions to create an environment of openness and trust.

While Rachel's focus is on inclusion and trust, her aim is to build a community where employees care about each other and encourage each other to do their best work. In turn, employees develop a feeling of connection to the organization. She creates conditions where the company can continue to nurture and cultivate mutuality, or a caring community, even after her work is completed.

In Sum

The narratives in this chapter illustrate strategies for building mutuality, which include:

- Foster connections—Be available for conversations and support.
- Make it safe to criticize. Make yourself available to hear employees' ideas and experiences.
- Acknowledge others—Show employees that you and the company care about them.
- Understand which communications work most effectively with your employees.
- Ask what your team needs in order to do their best work.
- Create clarity about roles and responsibilities.
- Give teams autonomy to solve problems and build solutions.
- Use recognition moments to help employees to progress in their careers.
- Always act in ways that promote employees' financial, physical, and mental well-being.
- Use measurement tools to assess the level of connection among your employees. This includes being racially and gender inclusive to produce higher engagement, better retention rates, greater profitability, improved ability to attract the best and brightest employees.

Reflective Questions

1. Reflecting on your own leadership, rate how well you express care toward your employees on a scale of one to five.

2. What lessons from the case studies can you apply to improve your rating?
3. What impact do you expect to have when you improve your ability to express care toward your employees?
4. Looking at your team, what do you know about each of your employees' lives outside of work?
5. What tactics are you using to create meaningful connections?
6. How does your team proactively get to know each other?
7. How do you ensure your organization is creating a shared experience of mutual understanding and acceptance?
8. How often do you individually check in with yourself?
9. What are you doing to confirm understanding of how your team feels?

CHAPTER 6

Ingenuity: Inventive Problem-Solving Using Toggling

CHAPTER 1 DESCRIBES THIS Core Differentiator, ingenuity, as the ability to invent novel solutions that serve the interests of many. This ability requires the leader to toggle between empathic and analytic understanding.

Beyond mere cleverness, ingenuity is the capacity to observe, interpret, and synthesize a lot of disparate information and then make the best decision for the individual and the whole. There is a connection element: the empathic. There is also a problem-solving element: the analytic. In combination, these two elements comprise ingenuity.

THE CORE DIFFERENTIATORS

The Sixth Level™

From Smelly Clothes to Saving Lives

By Megan Eddings

ENTREPRENEURSHIP FOUND ME IN a very odd way. One day, I was again facing a common household issue—smelly laundry—and the next, I was creating a business. I was tired of throwing away my husband's workout clothes because their stench assaulted my nose, breached my own clothes in the washing machine, and permeated my house. I searched for a solution, but after finding none, I decided to invent one.

Equipped with a background in chemistry and biochemistry from the University of Virginia, I researched why our clothes smell. With my "there is a solution to every problem" attitude, I invented Prema fabric. Prema is a sustainable, odor-resistant, antibacterial fabric, and it is 100 percent sourced and made in the US.

For me, manufacturing in the US was crucial, because I wanted every aspect of my supply chain to adhere to fair labor laws—no sweatshops. As I was the sole member of my company, the only way to accomplish this was to source and manufacture everything here. Surprisingly, I found it just as difficult to secure a quality domestic supply chain as it was to invent my fabric. Once again, my "there is a solution to every problem" attitude prevailed, and I found my suppliers.

My first official team member joined in 2018. In August 2019, we launched a company called Accel Lifestyle. Accel Lifestyle was created to exist as a fitness apparel brand using our proprietary Prema fabric. I never would have predicted that my business would grow so quickly. But it surged—virtually overnight.

Less than a year after we launched, we encountered another inflection point. I can tell you exactly where I was on March 20, 2020, when the United States shut down due to the pandemic. Stunned, I sat on my couch, deciding whether to turn my Prema fabric into face masks.

At the time, no one knew if the pandemic would last a couple of days or a couple of years. However, something bigger than me told me to take the risk and start making sample face masks. Fortunately, I had stored thousands of yards of Prema in our garage. All I needed was a team to help me.

Having to build a team instantly was a daunting hurdle. I had to find sewers in Houston to craft masks from our raw Prema goods. I also needed help driving thousands of yards of fabric and thousands of yards of elastic to these sewers all around Houston. In addition, I knew I would eventually need an all-hands-on-deck team to help me pack the masks for shipment.

It occurred to me that many of my friends who worked in the restaurant or retail business were laid off because of COVID. The timing of their needs and mine seemed to align absolutely perfectly. I had lived in Houston for sixteen years and built various friend groups during that time. However, the friends who came to work with me did not know each other, and I did not know if they would work well together. But I moved forward, bringing them to my "shop," also known as my living room, and it proved to be one of the most beautiful experiences of my life.

I let every hospital know we had the capacity to make Prema face coverings, and within the first two weeks of the US shutdown, I received purchase orders for about forty thousand masks. These coverings would protect people from the highly contagious and often deadly COVID-19 virus, and I felt immense pressure to turn the mask orders around as quickly as possible. I realized the only way I could accomplish this was if my friends worked continuously, sometimes seven days a week. Long hours were not the only problem, however. None of my friends had a background in pattern making, health care, or quality control, and I needed to train them. Fast!

I had to do something to make this improvised team successful. Their success would have a direct impact on saving lives.

At this time, the pandemic had caused great fear, stress, and sadness. People were losing their jobs, and many could not see loved ones. In addition, the daily death toll was staggering. I wanted to make everyone I worked with feel truly valued, so I offered to pay twenty dollars per hour, a wage much higher than many had been earning. I was happy to pay that rate, as I needed their help, and previous earnings from Accel enabled me to support that level of payroll. It was my way of expressing gratitude for the success of my business. But I knew I needed to do something more than pay high wages to keep spirits up and motivate my friends to dedicate long hours to my business. I had to create a safe, fun, welcoming, and purpose-centric environment. So I continuously added activities to build a positive culture.

Music

Who doesn't love music? Every single day, anywhere between ten and thirty of my friends came over at 8:30 a.m. I blared music through my home's surround sound so it made them feel like they were walking into a party. My goal was to keep the mood as joyful as possible. Music ranging from Drake to Beyonce to Whitney Houston welcomed them to work.

Lunch

Because restaurants were doing takeout only, we ordered lunch locally each day. Every morning, I chose a different person to pick the location. I believed it was important for everyone to feel we were giving back, and I smiled at the enthusiasm this small task instilled, realizing it might be the biggest decision he or she made that day.

TikTok Dances

TikTok had just come out with dances for people to learn and replicate, and I knew most of my friends enjoyed it. It was not about being a great dancer; it was about letting loose and having fun. A few times a week, we took a thirty- to sixty-minute dance break. Someone learned a new TikTok dance and taught it to us, and we performed and recorded it. Many days I was reluctant to devote a full hour to dancing for fear of falling behind in our workload, but I also knew the dance hour inspired levity and added to everyone's positive mental health. Thus, day after day I draped my measuring tape, my go-to dance accessory, around my neck as if it were a cape of leadership. Then I proclaimed myself the "positivity enthusiast." Instead of falling behind, our overall productivity continuously increased.

Community

While we ate lunch, my team sat all over my kitchen, living room, and floor while we relaxed and chatted. I moved my office from the second floor to the kitchen table on the first floor to stay in proximity to the group. I sometimes joined in the lunch conversation, but even when I did not, I could hear the group talking. I am extremely fortunate and blessed that my friends represent a true community: all religions, races, sexual preferences, and identities. Many times I overheard them talk about specific challenges in their lives, both as adults and as children, and I reveled in the ensuing acceptance they displayed. Love, community, and safety prevailed in my living room during the pandemic, and no external force could divide us.

Giving Back

Besides making and packing masks for large health care institutions, we donated many as well. We gave to nursing homes, orphanages, schools, and more. I wanted my team to experience the value of what they were accomplishing in a very personal way. One day, I asked them each to pack up fifty to one hundred masks and put them in a box. I did not tell them where they were going. Then I asked them to choose any place in Houston and personally deliver them. I will never forget how my small ask lit up the entire room. Each person took this request very seriously. It was obvious they were feeling good about being part of a big picture that provided protection from a deadly disease, but this new task manifested joy. Mask deliveries were made everywhere from the local fire department to the local Houston Veteran Affairs Hospital.

How I Led

With two people leading a team of over thirty, I had no time to write down how I wanted to manage. I just went with my gut. However, my gut and my decisions to create a place of community, fun, and purpose stemmed from twenty-five years of experience working in a variety of business environments always led by men. Intuitively I knew their leadership styles would not work in my company, as their focus was never building a community centered around purpose and fun. I needed to lead with my own strengths.

Looking back, I realize not having time to sit down and formulate a plan was one of my greatest gifts. There was no time to overanalyze. All I knew was that I had to create a safe environment (when we were all ridden with fear) and create an atmosphere of confidence and productivity. And productive we were. We made approximately $2.5 million dollars from masks during the pandemic. I was able to put together the most incredible team I have ever experienced. And we provided a solution that helped save lives—all while remaining profitable.

From my first job as a papergirl in my neighborhood to my last job as a medical sales representative, I learned human beings share a common desire. All we want is to be seen, heard, and valued. This intrinsic need is the core of my style of leading and what allows me to learn from my team. By creating a space of openness and a place to thrive, no matter one's position in the company, everyone wins.

I never thought to ask anyone on my team how I made them feel while we worked during the pandemic. But I decided to reach out to a few for insight when writing this narrative. I thought it was important to see if my team members felt self-worth and accomplishment while working with me—one of my main goals.

Here's a short excerpt from Stewart Webb's response. He wrote:

Seeing Accel Lifestyle transition from a start-up in leisurewear to a multicontinent supplier of PPE and more was miraculous. Getting to be a part of it was truly a gift. None of it would have been possible if not for the small but dedicated team Megan assembled. When walking into the shop, also known as her living room, you became part of not only one of the most diverse teams I have ever been a part of but also one of the highest performing.

The key to it all—inclusion. Megan made you feel like you were with family. Knowing you could not only trust everyone on the team but that they had your back. It was truly a sense of togetherness, and we knew we could and would accomplish great things.

At the ripe old age of forty-one, and only a few years into my entrepreneurial journey, I cannot think of any greater compliment from someone on my team. Life is a journey for all of us. Some of us choose to be leaders, and with that role comes substantial responsibility. It's one I am honored to take on every single day.

Future Leadership Models Must Factor in Emotions at Work

By Jennifer J. Fondrevay

"YOU KNOW, A MAN would never write a book like the one you are writing," he said.

Puzzled, I asked, "What do you mean?"

"It would never dawn on a guy working in business to consider these things. The topics you cover in your book, like the emotional toll of business transformation and the 'stages of grief' employees can experience—that these would need to be discussed," he replied.

He added, "I agree leaders need to lead differently during a merger, acquisition, or any business transformation for that matter. But it hadn't dawned on me that people can lose sight of their value when the business is evolving and changing. I never considered how the emotions people experience can dramatically impact the success of the deal. That is why your book needs to be written."

This conversation sparked an epiphany. I'd been interviewing CEOs as research for the first book I was considering writing, called *NOW WHAT? A Survivor's Guide for Thriving Through Mergers & Acquisitions*.

After *NOW WHAT?* was published and reached bestseller status, I wondered how I ever could have doubted whether to write it. Yet at the time of my conversation with the previously mentioned CEO, the book's potential success wasn't obvious. Our conversation revealed the reason: the *leadership lessons* I highlighted weren't obvious to others—especially men.

What was apparent to me, but which the CEO underscored was not for most, was that business transitions are emotional journeys for employees. The bigger the transformation, the greater the feelings and the longer the journey. They are not emotions we are used to experiencing at work, especially as leaders in business who are taught to embody confidence, certainty, and conviction. These are the traits of leaders we tend to follow—leadership characteristics typically associated with men.

Yet in times of business transition, confidence, certainty, and conviction can morph into self-doubt, questioning, and fear. These emotions are driven by not knowing what to expect as transformation is set in motion. While some employees get excited by the possibilities of change and are on board from the get-go, the majority will resist, holding on to what they know. Can you lead people when they experience feelings that spur resistance? Yes, you can, but leadership requires a change in tools from your traditional leadership tool kit.

You start with being vulnerable and acknowledging the emotional aspect of the business transition. People need to know you understand their struggle. You meet them where they are. An empathetic leadership style recognizes that embracing change is an emotional journey. When you ignore the signs of employees' varying emotional states and don't address them, you lose people. They check out—either mentally or physically, heading out the company door.

I know this to be true because I lived it. An empathetic leadership style had *not* been role modeled by most of the leaders during the post-deal integration I experienced. The traditional command-and-control version of leadership was the norm, a style of leadership, I observed, that was less than successful. As the CEO I interviewed noted, it simply wouldn't dawn on male leaders to address the emotional aspects of change. He reinforced *NOW WHAT?* had to be written if we had any hope of improving the 70 to 90 percent failure rate of merger and acquisition (M&A) deals.

On the Richter scale of business transition, M&A deals are the *tsunami* of change and uncertainty. The failure rate has endured because M&A deals are complex. I've witnessed the negative impact of M&As on companies as an advertising executive, and I've lived through three multibillion-dollar deals. I have been on all sides of the deal equation: acquired, acquirer, and acquired by private equity (its own unique event). Each of my deals taught me critical lessons about leading people through change:

1. You may question your sanity as you experience an array of emotions through a business transformation. It's important to remember you are not alone. Change is a process, not a linear path, and your willingness to remain open about your emotions enables you and others to reach a place of acceptance.

2. You may see a different side of people when they are uncertain about the future and afraid for their job. Your role is not to judge them but to understand the emotions that drive their actions and to role model the behavior you wish to see.

3. You may doubt your value as the business metrics for success evolve and you aren't clear how your skills and expertise will match up. Knowing your value—that is, really understanding and owning your unique gifts—gives you the confidence to embrace uncertainty. When you know your value, you see change as an opportunity to contribute your expertise.

During my M&A journeys, I was desperate for a book that explained the changes in people I observed. Most books I found concentrated on the art of the deal. They focused on when to pursue a deal, how to get the best valuations, which type of advisor to get the deal done, and so on. Other than William Bridges's seminal guide, *Surviving Corporate Transition*, most books were written by men focused on the capital gains of business transformation. Few were written for the people navigating postdeal changes. *NOW WHAT?* presents the female version of an M&A deal, written from the point of view of a survivor.

As tempting as it was, I didn't want *NOW WHAT?* to be a vendetta book or a tell-all of my crazy M&A experiences. The message needed to serve as a leadership model for how to succeed in M&As, not only how to navigate the postdeal environment but how to lead people through change and uncertainty. I intentionally rebuked what I'd experienced in my M&A journeys. I refuted the purely academic or consultant models that looked at everything through a logical lens without addressing the emotional toll of ongoing change.

My lived experience propelled the strategies I proposed. I had felt the emotions I wrote about. I had seen the change in behavior of people I thought I knew. I had questioned my value and wondered how I might find my way forward.

I knew any M&A leadership model also had to serve leaders on the front lines: the leaders who aren't in the room when the deal is made but who are burdened with the execution. I had been this leader, and based on my experience, frontline leaders most need a road map to understand and navigate the emotional aspect of change.

My first step in developing an M&A leadership model was to illuminate people's thinking around emotions at work. Borrowing from Elisabeth Kübler-Ross's groundbreaking work on the stages of grief experienced by terminally ill patients, I described how grief can manifest at work after a M&A deal. Similar to dying patients, people may "mourn the future that won't be" as their company evolves through the business transition.

As Kübler-Ross identified, the grief stages—denial, anger, bargaining, depression, and acceptance—are heartfelt emotions. They can be tough to discuss for many of us—especially in business. To help people understand their emotions and feel comfortable expressing them, I brought them to life—literally—through illustration.

The Stages of Grief

Denial   **Anger**   **Bargaining**   **Depression**   **Acceptance**

Each stage of grief is illustrated with an employee engaging with "the company" (represented by a building) to bring an M&A's unique grief journey to life. There is a chapter devoted to each stage, describing how that emotion manifests during a deal and exposing the emotion for what it is—part of a natural process. Humanizing the stages of grief and normalizing a person's feelings is critical and foundational to my model. Readers need to recognize there were expected patterns and know they are not alone in their experience. By vividly portraying the grief that can occur during business transformations, my leadership model helps employees:

- Understand why they are experiencing these emotions
- Appreciate they are not alone
- See their way toward acceptance

Leaders I've worked with reveal this creative approach to an M&A's grief stages "saved their lives." They thought they were "going mad" until they read my book or heard me talk and recognized these feelings were not unusual. Additionally, executives I've consulted for confide that my model revealed how emotions can negatively influence any transformation effort. Understanding how to help their employees manage these emotions made them better leaders. Men tell me, "I'm so glad you made it okay to talk about these things and equally showed us how to resolve them."

As a leader who experienced the emotional roller coaster of change, I knew it wasn't enough to simply help people identify their emotions. *People equally needed help finding their way toward acceptance.* To do this, I built on William Bridges's concept of the "neutral zone." This is a period in employees' M&A journey when they transition from the old way of doing things and adapt to and accept a new way. I tapped into the power of music to guide people through this zone.

The idea to use music came as I recalled how I'd navigated the emotional times of early boyfriend breakups! Listening to the Beatles, AC/DC, Anita Baker, Frank Sinatra, and Fleetwood Mac helped me process my emotions. Research has shown that *music helps us process our feelings* and can move us toward a place of acceptance. Using music and creating a Spotify playlist specifically became my leadership tool for helping people get to acceptance.

The playlist, called *From Denial to Acceptance*, includes songs for each stage of grief and taps into the power of music to help people process their feelings. In my leadership workshops, employees create their own playlist, selecting songs that best describe:

- How they felt when they first heard the deal news
- How they feel currently
- How they want to feel in three months

This interactive music exercise playfully enables employees to articulate their feelings. I've run sessions where participants couldn't wait to shout out: Miley Cyrus's *Wrecking Ball*, the Beatles' *Yesterday*, or Johnny Paycheck's *Take This Job and Shove It*. In each instance, participants named songs to describe how they'd previously felt or what they felt in the moment. When they chose a song for how they wanted to feel in the future, the act of doing this helped them see a way forward. It accelerated their ability to be a key contributor to the company's future.

I realize my leadership approach is unconventional. Some might say unorthodox. By creating a Spotify playlist and using illustrations to help people navigate the M&A stages of grief, I shifted the traditional command-and-control leadership model toward one where empathy and connection played a bigger part. My leadership experience taught me that you need to meet people where they are in their journey to help them move forward.

Shedding light on what holds people back in the face of change is central to my leadership model. When employees are fearful for their job, you may see another side of them. They can go into "survival mode," where they do or say things they might not normally do. I witnessed this throughout my M&A experiences. The next critical piece of the model was to prepare leaders for this reality and to show how people's personalities can shift in the face of change.

Pulling from my acquisition experiences as well as sixty-plus executive interviews, I identified ten M&A personas. From the Know-It-All to the Former Rock Star (shown here), the Missing-in-Action to the Ostrich, each persona brings to life the behavior changes we may witness in people. In keeping with my mission to humanize the M&A experience, each persona was brought to life through illustration.

During research for *NOW WHAT?,* the illustrations routinely sparked lively conversations with the executives I interviewed. The caricatures capture personas they had witnessed and worked with, and telling stories about them gave the executives a way to share their lessons learned. These lessons were integrated into my work and leadership model: a model that reinforces the human emotions and behavior triggered by uncertainty and how we help each other through the change.

As a survivor of three multibillion-dollar M&As, I've witnessed the consequences of not paying attention to the people piece in deal strategy. The people part does not simply represent the culture integration needs or change management piece but the emotional impact of change and uncertainty for people. My M&A leadership model makes the people piece the cornerstone of deal strategy.

Time and again, as I work with leaders and their teams, guiding them on how to lead people through the M&A journey, I hear a similar statement. Repeatedly leaders say, "I wish I had known about you and your model for my last deal. It would have saved us so much anguish and money!"

Yes, there is another way. A better way to do M&As. As a female leader, I'm doing my best to spark a different approach and to make smoother transitions happen—one book sale, keynote, and workshop at a time.

My Inner Journey to Outward Leadership

By Sucheta Jain

Finding My Inner Voice

I was twenty-one years old when I left my extended family in India and arrived in the United States to continue my studies at Rutgers University. Even though I had helpful professors and kind classmates, I struggled to communicate and connect with the people around me. No one looked like me, and I couldn't understand anyone through their American accents.

One day, I sat on my bed in my dorm room and cried. I felt different, and different felt bad and isolating. I was too young and new to the US to appreciate the beauty of my differences. So I sat alone in my foreign surroundings and released months of sadness, loneliness, and depression. It didn't fix anything, but I did feel better. After twenty minutes, a calm settled over me. *But inside we're all the same*, my inner voice said.

My inner voice has driven me ever since. It strengthens and expands my connections (my family and friends know I will bring a friend home every time I attend a retreat, conference, or workshop). My inner voice heightens my curiosity. It teaches me how to listen to people. And it imbues me with trust and faith in humanity.

Founding Our Company Our Way: Beyond Technology

In 1992 my husband Shail and I cofounded a software company, Farragut Systems, Inc (formerly Intelligent Information Systems, Inc), where I served as the chief operating officer. I didn't come from a family of businesspeople. I had no experience running a company or managing a software team. Prior to Farragut, I worked as a software developer for six years with Eastman Kodak and Data General Corporation (now Dell EMC). I didn't start Farragut because I loved technology—in fact, technology had become less and less interesting to me as my career matured. I wanted to serve in a more direct role with customers, and I wanted to help our customers become better providers to *their* customers.

Four years after we started Farragut, businesses around the world began panicking about Y2K. Moving from two-digit year '99 to '00, experts feared, would wreak havoc on computer systems ranging from airline reservations to financial databases to government systems. We had ten people on staff. I knew Y2K was a unique growth opportunity for our business, but I also knew the wave could wipe us out if we didn't catch it just right. We were a young, unproven company, and I was a petite Indian woman in a field dominated by men. How would I sign new customers? Where would I find more people to help us with bigger projects? How would I earn everyone's *trust*?

When we set out to solve the impending Y2K problem, I was new to marketing, sales, customer relations, hiring, training, and project management, but I was confident in our people and methodology. Our methodology was solid, but it was also untested and risky.

Every day, I phoned long lists of CIOs. "You don't have to sign on for the full project," I told each one. "Let our people come to your office for a planning study. Then you can decide." I understood their challenges and had faith in our solution. I wasn't selling. I was *partnering* with them to solve a problem. That's how I found our new customers.

With new customers, we needed more resources. There was an acute shortage of software professionals due to the demand, so I decided to hire and train computer science graduates from NC State, UNC, and Duke. Unfortunately large companies like Oracle, Microsoft, and IBM had the same idea, and they flooded universities across the country. I asked myself, "Where can I find people to complete the work we have in our pipeline? What do I really need? Who do I need?"

When I arrive at an obstacle, I never give myself room to get stuck. Anxious? Of course. Stuck? No. Just because I don't have a solution doesn't mean there isn't one. Usually the answer is already simmering. All it takes is one friendly nudge from the universe—a reminder of something I read or something a colleague said. I resolve most new problems by combining old solutions and past experience with common sense.

I knew to complete the work, I needed logical thinkers, problem solvers, creative minds, and open learners. I focused on recruiting math and physics graduates and community college enrollees who studied software programming. My interview process was thorough and evaluative. *I was interested in what candidates were capable of more than I cared about their current skill set.*

Once I hired the team we needed, I concentrated on creating a comfortable workplace. I didn't know how to be a manager or establish a healthy company culture. I had experienced good managers and bad managers in the past, and I remembered how both made me feel. I wanted our employees to feel the way I did under my good managers, so I did what they did.

Not long after I was hired at Eastman Kodak, during a review of my work, my manager had smiled and said, "I knew there was some good design in there, and there it is." In every review, he highlighted the positives in my work and taught me how to make my code better.

I was assigned a new department head a few months later. The new manager scheduled a thirty-minute introductory meeting with each of the one hundred employees in my department. I was so impressed by the immediate one-on-one connection he established. The training, mentorship, and community support I'd experienced at Eastman was what I aspired to create for our team at Farragut.

I learned to pay attention, and I learned what our employees needed by paying attention.

One Monday morning at Farragut, I noticed a young, single mother looking for something to eat in our office kitchen. She had been too busy caring for her home and daughter over the weekend to care for herself. So we started providing Monday breakfast every week for all employees. When an employee got married, we invited their new spouse to the office to celebrate with our team. On work anniversaries, we presented employees with special gifts from the company. In our weekly pizza meetings, our team bonded over new babies, birthdays, work anniversaries, and company achievements. From the beginning, we established a policy of transparency with employees and customers about company finances. We continue these important traditions and practices to this day, because it all matters. It's all connected to the work we do every day for our customers.

When I think about all we built and achieved at Farragut, there's one story that always stands out. It was 1999. Al was the CIO at a Kentucky-based manufacturing business, and our software company was hired to prepare their mission-critical application for Y2K and facilitate a smooth transition into the new century. Al was on edge. Along with every CIO in the world, he worried how their enterprise program would handle the shift from December 31, 1999 to January 1, 2000. Would their entire system collapse over two digits? Al called me and said, "Sucheta, I'm considering canceling our project. I'm not confident your team will complete it successfully. I want to find another vendor."

"Give me until the end of the day, and I will call you back," I assured him. "I want to meet with my project manager and review our status." I knew our team was on track and capable of seeing his project through successfully. I needed to figure out how to convince Al.

When I called Al a few hours later, I told him to bring his team to our Durham office. "Spend two days with us. We'll do a thorough review of your project. If you're not satisfied, we will help you transition to another vendor." He agreed.

I was out of the office tending to a passport emergency for my daughter on the day they arrived. I didn't think twice about my absence. My daughter needed me, and I knew my project manager could handle it. Al's team came and left, highly pleased with our work and confident in our ability to see the project through. I learned that most people simply need someone to listen, reassure, and provide the right information in times of uncertainty.

By January 2000, Farragut delivered over a dozen Y2K projects successfully. We became a profitable $12 million company and grew from ten to one hundred employees in five years. I knew every employee's name and background and modeled that behavior for our managers. When managers completed annual performance reviews, I met with each employee to recognize their achievements, learn where they wanted to grow, and ask how I could help. Employee retention soared to 97 percent. Our people were highly engaged and happy. I always wanted to leave the world a better place than I'd found it. Now I had a team of people who wanted to do the same.

Once we grew inward, we grew outward as well. We expanded our impact beyond our office and into our southern Durham community through tutoring programs at Parkwood Elementary School, the

Food Shuttle's BackPack Buddies program, and the NC GreenPower initiative.

My Inner Harmony

Our synergy at Farragut reminds me a lot of jazz. I fell in love with jazz the first time I heard it—the distinct but equally important sound of each musician and their instrument, their freedom to deviate because they know the rest of the ensemble will adjust, accommodate, and complement, makes it special. Our employees possess the same mutual trust and understanding. Our company shines because our people shine, and our people shine because we encourage them to express every facet of their personality. We're not in the music business, but like with jazz, we create more together than we ever could apart.

Before I was a leader, I was many other things—an immigrant, a minority, a woman, a wife, a mother, a daughter. Before I was a leader, many people led the way for me. I didn't become a leader because I wanted to be in charge. I became a leader because I liked being with people more than I liked sitting at my computer. In my experience, leadership is as simple as doing what I feel called to do and inviting people to do it with me. One idea, one project, one year at a time.

In the last five years, I've shifted to a high-level advisory position with Farragut in order to pursue a more community-minded role as a life coach. I teach my clients how to navigate personal and professional obstacles, discover what fulfills them, and trust their inner voice. I want them to find their own purpose and peace by realizing the solution to any obstacle is already within them. And when they're struggling to find the answer, the simplest and most powerful thing to do is: pause, breathe, and listen.

The Strategic Thinking Shift

By Meghan Juday

MY FIRST YEAR AS Chairman of the Board of Directors for our fifth-generation family-owned business ended up rocky. Three weeks after I stepped into the chairman role, COVID hit. Our worldwide manufacturing plants were located in COVID hot spots, but shutting down was not an option because we were an essential business. In the beginning, we struggled with finding the best way to keep our employees safe as protocols and information kept changing. It was a challenging time, but our company values were always about putting our people before profits, so we found a way to make it work.

Business as usual during COVID was not an option, nor was operating our board as if the business were going to stay the same forever. As the world changed, it became clear that we needed new strategic direction and fresh ideas from the board to help guide us into the future. A board should exist to provide strategic oversight that helps management prepare for shifts in the industry, technological advances, or major challenges. So, I decided, after more than a hundred years in operation and sixty years of having a corporate board, we needed to make some changes. It was time to think about risk and opportunity in a whole new way.

Governance excellence is a journey, not a destination. Boards are constantly evolving, improving, bringing on new skills and perspectives, and shedding programs no longer relevant to the company's forward-looking mission. However, shifting and transforming to adapt to the business evolution requires a significant investment in change.

In our case, every aspect of the board had to be identified, evaluated, and redefined to support our goals of providing strategic oversight. We had to look at everything—from presentations to agendas—to move the group onto a more intentional path. And we had to ensure that the board was composed of members who could help us carry forward this deliberate vision. By pivoting to a strategic board, we knew we would create a more meaningful role for the group driving the affairs of the company and could provide better overall guidance, support, and direction for everyone.

In preparation for the upcoming changes, I connected one-on-one with each director to help them understand the reasoning behind the change in expectations. I shared articles and research to help everyone see and embrace the vision. I knew not everyone would feel comfortable with these changes, but I wasn't about to go back to the old way of doing things just to appease the few. The bigger picture—that the company needed a strategic board—was driving every decision I made.

As I began to communicate this change in direction to our board members, there was a shift in dynamics. What had felt like a supportive and collaborative environment suddenly seemed less stable. I started to feel the weight of being the only woman in the room and the youngest person on the board. It was nothing overt, just a change in the air. However, I was committed to turning our board into a strategic partner for the company and wasn't about to let this atmosphere shift detour a necessary move.

It helped that I carried a reputation as someone who was always prepared, did her research, and made thoughtful decisions. Several other people, including the nominating and governance committee chair, the CEO, and a few of the family directors, supported me and the direction we wanted to go. That allowed our board to do the work it needed to do despite the chaos of the pandemic and our internal struggles with change.

We took a multipronged approach to changing duties and roles. First, we developed a spacious agenda by being judicious about discussions in the boardroom versus initiating a board committee. Only those items that needed the consideration of the entire board were reviewed in meetings. Each session had an open agenda item, allowing the board to embark on wide-ranging and sometimes deep conversations. We also implemented a consent agenda, which greatly sped up the motions process. This allowed us to focus our boardroom time on those items that made a difference. Each meeting now included an executive session at both the beginning and end of the meeting to allow the directors to speak freely and off-the-record, and with and without management present.

Effective use of board committees is one of the best ways to make room in the board agenda. Boards have much to do in a limited time frame, usually only a few hours up to a day or two. Committees, however, can meet whenever they want. They also have a more modest annual agenda and a manageable group size, making scheduling meetings and taking on bigger projects, like executive compensation, much easier. As we moved more items out of the boardroom and into committees, we had to restructure our committees to take on more work. Each committee charter was revamped to have bigger program oversight and detailed reporting in addition to their standard duties of nomination, governance, audit, and compensation. These additional responsibilities included ESG (enterprise, social, and governance), cybersecurity, risk, and culture. This meant committee members couldn't gloss over a preprinted report. They had to get hands-on and know about the issues they were working on to make informed decisions.

Management moved from presenting 80 to 90 percent of the meeting materials to board members to about 30 percent. The directors now spent time reviewing the board book before sessions so they had time to think strategically about the information rather than making fast decisions on the spot. Also, by cutting back on repetitive management presentations, our board was able to dive much deeper into the topics and issues that mattered most. This left ample time for dialogue with management at the board meeting.

These days, we are focused primarily on strategy and future outlooks rather than the minutiae of previous quarters. Board discussions do not veer into operational matters unless there is a crisis.

Along with our new format, we've also changed our board materials to focus on providing more valuable information prior to upcoming discussions rather than producing a "data dump" of all the previous quarter's results. An appendix with vital data to review includes board minutes, resolutions, detailed financials, and general updates. Still, unless someone voices a concern, it does not become a significant focus of our discussion. During discussions, we capture the directors' suggestions and recommendations during each board meeting and report progress at each successive session. This is a crucial step, reassuring the board that management is considering their advice and allowing us to see how our decisions are affecting the company more consistently.

My mission disrupted the group thinking that had been part of the board for many years. It was a big shift for many people but ultimately one that hugely benefited the company. By shaping the board into a strategic thinking group, we acted as better fiduciaries for our shareholders and enhanced the value the board brought to the management team. These two components drove shareholder value creation because we gave the company tools to move more nimbly and become future-focused.

It's hard for a board to be effective without the right people in the room. Even with the best governance, your board probably won't make substantial changes without effective directors. We were fortunate to have talented individuals who had served for many years, including when I'd served with them as a director and vice-chair. However, we would not have been able to make these changes if the composition of our board hadn't changed. Four directors have left, leaving room for four fresh thinkers. We've gone from a board comprised of one woman and eight men when I started to a board including three women and four men. We will continue to look for diverse directors as we add to our ranks.

With that shift in dynamics and people, our perspectives have also evolved. Facilitation is intentional, so all voices are welcomed. We also made a significant investment in developing relationships and building a solid culture in the boardroom. This includes moving to in-person committee meetings, board dinners, and a full-day board meeting. We invite anyone presenting to the board and high potential employees to join us for the board dinner the night before.

The board's significant work in the last few years has built trust with the management team and our directors. Without this, we wouldn't have vulnerability, curiosity, respect, or support. These necessary ingredients allow the board to support our management team and help execute a winning strategy.

Implementing these changes with the support of the rest of the board and management team has resulted in meetings that are getting better and better each quarter. The conversations are wide-ranging and curious, and they build on each other's ideas. We've created an environment where each director is respected for their unique talents and insights.

We now find ourselves walking into board meetings thinking differently. We still believe we know how the conversations and decisions will go, but then we find ourselves group-strategizing unique solutions that none of us would have come up with on our own. That is the true value of a diverse board, one brave enough to change how things have always been done and embrace a new way of thinking and moving forward.

Sustainability through Partnership

By Sharon Weinstein

THE RUSSIAN FEDERATION, UKRAINE, Moldova, Belarus, and Romania share borders and headlines each day. They likewise share a unique history, one in which countries, once a part of the Soviet Union, were granted independence in the 1990s. Afterward, members of the medical community, once linked by a common country, were no longer able to communicate with their former colleagues through international conferences and symposia. Nurses were not included in learning opportunities. They were primarily female, lacked authority, and were relegated to the "middle-level" label.

I wish I could take you back to 1992, when I was a member of the team responsible for creating a new health care infrastructure for these countries. Throughout the New Independent States (NIS) and Central and Eastern Europe (CEE), I led the initiative to build a community of like-minded peers, and what a privilege it was. The slate was wide open, and the academic service health care partnership held the key. I used my thirty-five-year nursing platform to educate, engage, and empower others.

I met with NIS and CEE teams identified by their governments who were eager to begin—enthused about partners who shared their vision of better care, education, and results. Many had existing relationships with US colleagues through Sister Cities International. This made it easy to match sister cities such as Atlanta in the state of Georgia and Tbilisi in the country Georgia.

Funding came from the United States Agency for International Development (USAID), and in-kind contributions of time, talent, and resources came from US health systems. Through my nursing network, I identified US professionals who shared their time and expertise via peer-to-peer institutional partnerships. They created models of care, trained health care providers, and strengthened professional societies and regulatory bodies. How? When I had a relationship with a nurse leader, I simply asked. Absent an existing relationship, I asked my colleagues for introductions. Selling them on need was easy.

US nurse colleagues trusted me based on established relationships through professional societies and my knowledge of cross-cultural health care. They recognized an opportunity to travel abroad, make a difference, and lead change. They volunteered readily. Pushing aside their egos, they embraced the chance to chair subgroups and share their own success stories.

And our NIS and CEE colleagues trusted me, even though I was a nurse, because of the word "director" on my business card. That label denoted that I directed a global health care network and, as a USAID designee, was responsible for budgets and outcomes. I would deliver.

I controlled the money, and a component of our program had to include nursing reform. I created a process including inputs and outputs to meet funding agency requirements and allow local facilities to meet their respective goals, potentially clinical care or medical and nursing school curriculum. The new first lady of Armenia, Lucia Ter-Petrosyan, invited me to accompany her to a local orphanage. She shared her concerns about the future of those who, at fifteen, aged out. She envisioned a school of nursing to fill the pipeline for in-country nurses. Brimming with ingenuity, I listened to the goals, visited potential sites, and developed the school. The teenagers from the orphanage became our first cohort of nursing students in Yerevan. We were on a roll, and we were building momentum!

Challenging Authority

As a kid growing up, I was told, "You'll never amount to a damn thing. You should just learn to type."

So I learned to type, and so much more. I learned to challenge authority and developed the change I wanted to see. I learned to create possibilities, and that lesson has remained with me for a lifetime.

I found my voice and my secret sauce through an infusion cannula and quickly transitioned from novice to expert. I emerged as national president three years after joining a professional society. I discovered my purpose, and I had a vision.

In 1984, I taught infusion therapy in the former Soviet Union through the People-to-People Organization. Travel included a group visa to a country that encompassed eleven time zones and had lots of rules. This was different. Now, male-dominated independent countries demanded that potential collaborators demonstrate competency through a medical degree. Female physicians were acceptable. But what about me? I was a woman, but not a doctor. A master's-prepared nurse who had crossed multiple borders and director of the office of international affairs, I facilitated cross-country relationships between my five thousand US hospitals and their global counterparts. But was it enough?

When a Russian colleague said, "In our country, all things are possible—not everything is probable," I adopted my childhood mantra and decided to make the improbable possible!

To me, there was no box. I was willing to do what was needed. Consistent with the nursing process of assessment, diagnosis, planning, implementation, and evaluation, I began with an on-site needs assessment. Our team identified the status quo, prioritized learning needs, then developed and implemented a model that could be evaluated, replicated, and sustained.

With defined goals for each country, we built community through structured work groups or nursing task forces leading the way. Comprised of US nurse leaders who collaboratively created curriculum and educational method and model enhancements, they provided a forum for the exchange of ideas and lessons. The nursing agenda focused on education, practice, and leadership.

Next, I opened nursing resource centers (NRCs) in twenty-six countries equipped with computers, textbooks, and simulation labs. To date, over 7,100 nurses have used the NRCs for continuous learning and refinement of clinical skills. As a team, we developed fifteen nursing associations, including the federation model, All-Ukrainian Nursing Association. Beyond time-honored soft skills like compassion and caring, this profession addressed societal needs beyond borders through communication, decision-making, and leading through uncertainty. All critical skills.

INLI: A Sustainability Success Story

Building on the base of successful practices, curriculum, and nursing associations, I created the International Nursing Leadership Institute (INLI). This unique, year-long, three-session experience was designed for nurse leaders to change their status, gain respect, and lead for the future. Using adult learning principles and an interactive approach, we generated a cadre of developing leaders for developing nations.

The strategy could be implemented in any emerging country and with any discipline, but our targets were NIS and CEE nurses. Unlike their colleagues in the US and Western Europe, nurses in these regions were viewed as an extension of the physician. They were seen as middle-level workers rather than as independent professionals. Lack of standards, the absence of nurses in positions of power and influence, low status, insufficient pay, high turnover, and low morale all presented an opportunity for meaningful change. Thus evolved our partnership model—and with it, nursing's future.

Because NIS and CEE senior nurses have always taken a back seat to physician administrators within their respective institutions, it was essential that nurses develop skills associated with senior leadership roles. The partnership model helped identify emerging nurse leaders in each country. We advocated for our foreign colleagues, anticipating a transformation. Over a three-year period, these early leaders became presidents and executive directors of local nursing associations and chief nurses of their respective health ministries. The INLI format satisfied the next phase of the leadership model—the ability to sustain the successes and disseminate them to a larger pool of practitioners.

Instruction was active, student-centered, and based on the learners' goals. We created an environment with "real-life" applications for the content, built on experiences, and promoted self-esteem. A series of leading management books was used to develop the curriculum. Students and faculty, in full costume, acted out the stories. For example, the parable *Who Moved My Cheese?* (Johnson 1998) encouraged students to create contingency plans and expect change. Students created a maze and moved through it to reach their destinations, facing multiple obstacles along the way, including a shortage of "cheese" (supplies).

The book *The Oz Principle* (Connors, Smith, and Hickman 1998) told students they could be or do whatever they wanted—if they wanted it badly enough. The author contended that, like Dorothy and her companions in *The Wizard of Oz*, most people in the corporate world have the power within themselves to get the results they need. Instead, they behave like victims of circumstance. Faculty became the characters and led the students through the story, ending in Dorothy using the power within her to return home.

The book *Goldilocks on Management* (Mayer and Mayer 1999) featured a series of revisionist fairy tales. A message from *Chicken Little* reminded students that they could control rumors with timely, accurate, and effective communication. Costumes, props, and teamwork enriched the course content.

To apply interventions, INLI students participated in thought-provoking exercises, worked collaboratively in cross-country groups, and completed reflective journal entries. They role-played and learned to adapt to change. Students had to develop a local ministry and institution-approved project, which was critiqued for evidence of critical thinking. Core content included project development, communication skills, change-barrier management, systems thinking, negotiation skills, and conflict resolution. Our goal was to prepare resourceful, independent next generation leaders who could influence nursing's future and speak with a collective voice.

Armed with the talent and tools needed to advance in their respective nursing careers, the first class graduated in June 2000. Four graduates were selected to serve as faculty for the next round of workshops. The majority (72 percent) of INLI graduates believed the program had helped them in changing their status and gaining respect from their physician colleagues. Almost all (87 percent) felt that graduating from INLI helped them recognize their professional and leadership capabilities. Of the respondents, 34 percent received a promotion at their workplace during or after the training. Three graduates were promoted to the position of head nurse. Two became chief nurse and deputy chief. The rest received new titles such as chairs of the nursing department, lab specialists, and district leader nurses.

From INLI to the Global Education Development Institute

When USAID funding dried up, we explored other ways in which to fund our initiatives. We developed the Global Education Development Institute (GEDI), a grassroots 501(c)(3) program whose goal is to follow Florence Nightingale's path leading to global health. As pioneers, we are twenty-first century Nightingales. We aim to make a collective difference that will affect future generations of people across the globe. Today, in every corner of the world, nurses are recognized as key drivers in care delivery.

Outcomes Achieved

A move toward nurse faculty developed after years of basic nursing education in the NIS and CEE countries viewed as vocational training rather than university-based. This led to a baccalaureate-level model. The philosophy of nurses teaching nurses quickly adapted, and pilot programs were developed in select countries. Faculty from the US were recruited to coteach standardized curriculum. The first BSN (Bachelor of Science in Nursing) graduation from Erebuni College of Nursing was celebrated by nurse colleagues, government officials, and even the medical community.

Nursing education then expanded from a two-year program to advanced training. Four-year baccalaureate nursing programs became commonplace. International nursing conferences extended the learning process.

Changes in clinical practice have evolved through updated guidelines, nursing standards, policies, procedures, and teaching models. Individual-centered care follows a care plan, promotes interdisciplinary communication, and enhances outcomes. Countries such as Kyrgyzstan and Russia have developed nursing roles for clinical nurse educators, clinical managers, and nurse teachers.

Unexpected Challenges

In creating the model NRCs, we underestimated physician interest in the materials, space, and access. Because they lacked the travel experience, they took control of the resource materials and centers in some Central Asian Republics, arguing that physicians, by virtue of their education, should have access to more than nurses.

Mobilizing Nursing's Future

Nurses today are empowered to be more resourceful and independent, think critically, educate colleagues, patients, and the community, manage departments, represent the profession to the public, and speak with one collective voice. In short, they are respected second-generation leaders.

Through the exceptional leadership of NIS and CEE nurse leaders, the discipline and practice of nursing have advanced in a multitude of ways with cross-country linkages. The impact of this work will reach far into the next century and serve as a foundation upon which even greater advancements will evolve. I've gone from giving nurses a voice to creating and sustaining their future. Thirty years later, these trusted next-generation leaders are replicating the ultimate sustainability story. They are mobilized for success.

INGENUITY LESSONS LEARNED

How did leaders in this chapter foster ingenuity?

While **Megan Eddings**'s company was founded on an ingenious solution to a common problem, her leadership approach also reveals ingenuity. When an opportunity to save lives and advance her business arose, she needed to quickly assemble and train a new workforce. Adding to the difficulty of finding this group, she knew that the workforce would need to work long hours in a comparatively small space. Megan had to find people and develop ways to keep these employees engaged and energized.

She did this by using novel approaches to leadership that appealed to both group and personal needs. She used music to start the day with a partylike atmosphere to encourage employees to interact in a positive environment. Lunchtime was transformed into a united effort to help the outside community and an opportunity for employees to learn about each other. Megan also dedicated time for dancing to help employees release tension, have fun together, and gain a chance to lead. Furthermore, Megan provided opportunities for employees to deliver their finished products to a place of their choice to experience the feeling of contributing to saving lives and align personally with the output of all their hard work.

Megan's leadership practices reflect ingenuity such that they had not been preplanned and each method helped build trusting bonds and a sense of community and purpose. Her ingenuity resulted in $2.5 million in revenue in a short period of time.

Ingenuity enabled **Jennifer Fondrevay** to write a book and develop a program to increase the success of mergers and acquisitions (M&As). She identified her own emotional patterns when she was undergoing M&As and noticed that others were displaying similar behaviors. She began to analyze these patterns, and three salient patterns emerged. She continued to explore these patterns through reading and interviews, and her insights and findings became the foundation of her book.

Effectively, Jennifer toggled between empathy for employees whose lives were upended by an M&A and analyzing their experiences to discover antidotes to their suffering. This process reflects ingenuity such that she used empathy and analysis to find creative solutions to a common problem.

Jennifer also demonstrated ingenuity in the methods she chose to educate her readers. She used cartoons to illustrate the process of grieving, helping employees address emotions they may have cared to ignore. Unlike most business books, she used music to help employees tap into and identify their emotions during an M&A and to guide them toward a more positive future. Furthermore, she used humor to help people identify and discuss interactions during the M&A that may have been disturbing or alienating.

Jennifer's ingenuity resulted in her book achieving number one on a bestseller list.

Sucheta Jain needed to be ingenious in order to seize a unique growth opportunity for her software business. At the end of 1999, all businesses were looking for help to address the threat of Y2K, but Sucheta needed to hire employees, find customers, and sell services. She did not have experience in any of these areas, and there was a shortage of talent with the skill sets she needed.

Sucheta met each challenge by listening to her inner voice and discovering solutions. When she interviewed potential employees, she assessed them for their ability to learn rather than their current skill sets. She offered potential customers complimentary planning services to demonstrate her company's trustworthiness and competence. And after a customer changed his mind about hiring her company, she provided two days of service with a promise to help him find another company if he was not pleased with their work.

Sucheta's ingenuity resulted in sales of $12 million, and this success led to more growth. Eventually the company expanded from ten employees to one hundred. She explains that her success reflects the inventiveness she hears when listening to jazz. She appreciates how musicians listen to each other, adjust, and create art. The key is that their work together surpasses what they can do individually. That principle guides her leadership.

Shortly after stepping into the position of chairman of the board of her family's fifth-generation business, **Meghan Juday** was faced with the responsibility of steering the company through the COVID pandemic. As she worked, it became apparent that the board needed more strategic and forward thinking. Meghan used her ingenuity to transform the board into a more proactive and responsive entity.

Meghan changed board roles and responsibilities and the structure of meetings and presentations. She allowed more time for in-depth discussions where board members could ask questions and build on each other's ideas. Critically, she replaced some board members to create a more diverse board with a wider range of skill sets.

Meghan demonstrated empathy when making these extensive board changes. She reached out to board members individually to address their concerns and share research and articles that motivated her decisions. This effort indicates the ethic of care when making changes that others may find unexpected or disquieting.

The changes Meghan implemented have led to more trust between management and the board, unique solutions to problems, and shareholder value creation.

After **Sharon Weinstein** completed her role in helping to create a new medical infrastructure in countries that were formerly part of the Soviet Union, she founded the International Nursing Leadership Institute (INLI). The objective of the program was to help nurses, particularly in Central and Eastern European countries. However, this program was designed not only to augment medical skills but to develop skills that would enable nurses to have a voice in health care policies.

The creation of this program illustrates inventiveness, but the pedagogy reflects empathy. Sharon used educational techniques that recognized each student's unique circumstances and goals and helped to build nurses' self-esteem. The program also utilized various teaching methods that recognized different learning styles.

As a result of Sharon's ingenuity, the nursing profession has been strengthened globally. Graduates of INLI have become presidents and executive directors of local associations. Some are chief nurses in their countries' health ministries. Others have received promotions to high-level leadership positions. INLI has continued for thirty years and has been influential in advancing the discipline and practice of nursing.

In Sum

The narratives in this chapter illustrate how leaders express ingenuity. Highlights include:

- Using playlists to engender a sense of understanding and alliance.
- Actively listening to employee needs and motivators.
- Creating a work environment that is comfortable for employees.
- Sharing forward-looking and strategic thinking with board members and staff.
- Creating more gender and racially inclusive environments.
- Creating affinity groups and activities that support both teamwork and autonomy.
- Using regular and creative recognition opportunities and providing frequent reviews.
- Letting employees define professional development opportunities.
- Building teamwork by doing challenge courses.
- Creating alliances that allow for a more collective voice.
- Building mutually invested teams interested in achieving the same results.
- Paying attention to employees bearing various emotional states and addressing them.
- Fostering a culture of curiosity.

Reflective Questions

1. When you noticed a "gap" in how something was being managed, what were you compelled to do and what did you hold back from doing?
2. Identify where ingenuity was used to solve a problem and speculate on subsequent long-term benefits.

3. Reflecting on your own leadership, think of a time when you listened to your inner voice with an ingenious solution and a time when you ignored it because the environment wasn't open to it.

CHAPTER 7

Justness:
Equity Is Nonnegotiable

CHAPTER 1 DESCRIBES THIS Core Differentiator, justness, as the mechanism for organizations and communities to operate optimally together, requiring fair and full representation, transparent and consistent procedures for ensuring due process, fostering a sense of belonging and cohesion, and ultimately allowing the freedom to pursue purpose.

Justness is a set of imperatives that require a universal commitment to an ethic of care and the tenets of fair and full representation. Justness is grounded in transparent and consistent due process, access to safety, and equitable pay. Justness is a framework for our collective responsibility to propel progress as well as repair and renewal. Upholding the rights of individuals while fostering environments conducive to growth and advancement ensures the well-being and prosperity of the larger community.

THE CORE DIFFERENTIATORS

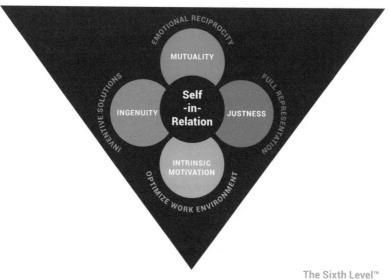

The Sixth Level™

The Executive Yogi

By Neeti Dewan

WHEN I WAS FOURTEEN, I moved to the United States from India. Moving to a new country, and to a city like Los Angeles, was a massive change for me and taught me at an early age what "change management" truly is. I desperately missed my favorite mentor, my grandfather. When I called him, I complained to him about how different it was here without my friends, my school, or my favorite fruit—mangoes.

I was feeling lost and adrift, uncertain in this new and strange environment. My grandfather told me to imagine my future and the path that would get me from where I was to where I wanted to be. Once I had done that, he told me, "Write it down; write it down."

That conversation transformed the way I handled the stress of the move and, later, how I led the people who worked with and for me. I began keeping journals that planned out my life, my goals, my missions going forward and used those to model the micro-thoughts and micro-actions I encouraged others to build as a way to overcome and achieve.

Even the mangoes I missed so much became a metaphor for how I lived my life and how I approached challenges. There is an old legend that says Buddha was given a mango grove so that he could find tranquility and a place to meditate beneath the cool, thick shade of the trees. I wanted to be calm and meditative; I wanted to feel that cool shade over my mind whenever things became too frustrating. As a leader, I also wanted to create more successful work environments so that the people who worked with and for me could find their own moment of tranquility, even in the midst of a crisis.

Doing that can sometimes mean going against the first instincts of the leadership above you, I found out early in my career. One day someone on my team made a huge mistake on a client project. Leadership was furious and demanded I come down hard on the person who had made the mistake and make sure this never happened again. I knew this typical agentic style of leadership was not going to work. It would be disruptive, leaving a lot of upset people in its wake. That was the opposite of productive and not the kind of leader I wanted to be.

Instead of yelling and screaming, I thanked the person for bringing the mistake to my attention. "We'll figure out together how to fix it," I said. "For now, I want you to focus your energies on everything else that needs to be completed for our clients."

Rather than being upset and distressed, the employee felt relieved and was able to concentrate on work. Leadership was outraged at my "bad leadership" in the handling of this crisis. I knew, however, that it wasn't a matter of life and death and that we could find a good solution if we operated from a place of calm. The employee finished the work that needed to be done, and a couple days later the two of us came up with a plan that fixed the problem. Because we remained calm, the fallout from the mistake was mitigated. The client's work got done, there was no disruption to the workflow, and we were able to have the mental breathing room to develop a good solution.

At a later point in my career, I was asked to step in as COO of a new business division that needed a massive turnaround. The negative margins made others in leadership panic. I knew a knee-jerk reaction could have long-term ramifications that could actually make things worse. We needed to know what we were dealing with before we developed a plan of action. We needed to do what I did in my journals—look at the entire picture, lay out a path forward, and list the actions that would get us there.

I took the next two months to assess all aspects of the business—the people, the clients, the processes, and the systems. I met with every single employee to determine who was a good fit and who wasn't so that I could bring in the right talent. Then I looked at the systems side of the business because I knew we couldn't go out and start selling if the foundation of the business was struggling. It turned out we had a gap in our technology that we needed to fill. Once those two key pieces of the business were fixed, we were ready to go sell.

In less than eighteen months, my team and I turned the business around, not just into the black but into double-digit positive margins. Through a combination of strategic decision-making, nurturing a culture of innovation, and leading with calm wisdom, we managed to take a once-struggling division and bring it back to life with increased sales, improved customer satisfaction, and a motivated workforce.

I'd known all along, however, that those results were possible. I had spent a lot of time thinking about the issues, understanding what was going on, and envisioning a successful future, which automatically built a list of the micro-actions we would need to take to get there. There was tremendous pressure from above to rush into triage and stop the bleeding, but that would have been a Band-Aid that didn't create a stronger base for the future.

It's important to take a breath, have that moment of calm, and give your mind room to assess before making any decisions. These are concepts I discuss in my books, *From Executive to Yogi in 60 Seconds* and *High-Level Leadership, Low-Level Stress,* and in my work as an executive yogi. In working with companies of all sizes, from start-up to Fortune 500, the first thing I do is take a step back and evaluate the people and resources. I talk to the team about where we want to go, not where we are, because when we are future-focused, we activate an invisible power that allows us to create our future "in this moment" and puts us in control of whatever is going on around us. Instead of stressing over a momentary detour or bemoaning a mistake in the past, we're able to cast our gaze down the road, toward the destination we are dreaming about. Our thoughts naturally become less frantic and more contemplative, opening the door to action.

I also create carefully curated project teams by intentionally pairing individuals with complementary skills so that they can learn from each other and capitalize on each other's strengths to work toward the common goal. Someone who is creative but has trouble staying on task can be a great partner for someone who is organized but lacks the courage to voice their thoughts. This creates a natural cross-pollination of ideas and increases both people's skill sets. These pairings can result in a remarkable transformation in previously floundering team members. They grow more confident, engaged, and motivated because we have created an atmosphere of mutual support and encouragement.

With start-ups especially, there is often a lot of chaos and uncertainty, which can result in rash decision-making. In those situations, finding tranquility is vital because it's easy to get caught up in the rush to grow or to react to fear of failure. If someone is feeling stressed, I encourage them to take a step back, reflect, and regain their composure. When they do this, their brain begins to form calmer micro-thoughts, which slowly bring them back to center.

It's also important to give people a way to express their concerns and fears, acknowledge their struggles, and provide them with a safe space for dialogue. To do that, I'll create one-on-one mentoring sessions between employees for many of the same reasons I intentionally pair people with complementary skills to work together on a project. These mentoring sessions are designed to allow each individual to seek their own answers and develop their problem-solving skills. It empowers them to become active participants in their goals, rather than someone above them who is always telling them what to do. That is the key to creating lasting change.

In my work with companies, I balance the wisdom of the East with the business genius of the West. The result is joyful leadership, which combines this approach from a calm state with the intentional actions that promote success for all. Joyful leadership is all about taking control of your mind and the chatter going on inside instead of reacting without thinking. When your whole being emanates joy, you rally the people around you to have fun and to enjoy every step in the process, good and bad. Whatever happens is simply part of the experience. If the people I am working with are stressing about something, I encourage them to find that calm space by taking a half hour break. Go for a walk, listen to music, or simply meditate with me. If they do that, they are guaranteed to return with a calmer, fresher perspective.

To maintain that kind of thinking as a leader, I spend a few minutes at the start of every day writing down my daily, midterm, and long-term goals. I break each of those goals into micro-actions for the day. That keeps me continually on a future-focused path, which prevents my thoughts from dwelling on the past or getting distracted by the present. This is a radically different approach from the typical react-first leadership model. The result is calmer teams, unhurried decisions, and careful strategies.

All that mental breathing room also gives you clarity. To me, clarity is more important than confidence. You can confidently do many things, but if they are the wrong things, you won't reach your goals. Instead, if you take the time to build micro-thoughts that are positive and solution-driven, the micro-actions you need to take will naturally unveil themselves. If you hit a setback, you simply take a pause to breathe, be still, and smile. Imagine yourself under the cool shade of a mango tree and fix your attention on the horizon. The road ahead will unfurl in front of you, one milestone at a time.

Accountability

By Elaine Russell Reolfi

WANT ACCOUNTABILITY? MAP A journey of clarity, alignment, and engagement.

Everyone knows what accountability is, right? "You do what you committed to do or face consequences." Is that how you see it?

When we focus on accountability by that definition, we're after the fact. We're waiting to reward or punish the outcome.

I've spent a career moving people to action as a writer, marketing professional, HR leader, and CEO. Whether I was equipping a sales team to sell products in a new market, creating talent management programs that aligned efforts toward a common goal, or taking a nonprofit through transformation, I always viewed those processes as a journey. The quest is to create clarity, alignment, engagement, and results. The fact is, we get the best outcome when we plan for it. And if we find ourselves speaking with frustration about a "lack of accountability," it's just too late.

That's where I found myself in April 2021. I'd taken the leap from public company executive to nonprofit behavioral health CEO. I joined a one-hundred-year old organization with 350 people and twenty programs in mental health, addiction recovery, and social support. It was a complex, underperforming organization with a smart and passionate team brimming with frustration over lack of results and arguing about the ways to fix it. The only thing they agreed on was the importance of the mission as they each defined it. The unified complaint was, "Our real problem is that there's no accountability around here."

I share with you now what I've lived since the moment I took on that role. We started from the beginning and equipped the team to succeed. That trek began by thinking like the people we were trying to motivate, drawing on their deep experience with our services, and outlining an action plan everyone could understand and participate in. So, let's think like a team member.

I want to understand my organization's purpose (and maybe even help define it).

Employees' belief in the organization is key to retention and engagement. That starts with very fundamental questions of "What are we here to do every day (our mission)?" and "What impact are we trying to make on the world over time (our vision)?"

Equally important is identifying the behaviors necessary for success (our values). By defining our values, we commit to how we're going to treat each other and our stakeholders.

Those are the foundational guideposts on which we establish strategic priorities and operational goals that start to directly answer the question of "To what are we holding ourselves accountable?"

I've led this work at a bearing company, a steel company, numerous nonprofit boards, and now in my role as a nonprofit leader. It doesn't matter the industry; success starts with these guideposts.

I have to know my role.

So often this is where things break down. In the large companies I've worked for, we had robust talent management systems that created the alignment between the organizational goals and individual objectives. In smaller organizations, we often don't have those systems. Regardless of the infrastructure, though, employees have to be clear on what their responsibility is to drive the mission forward, as well as the roles of others in doing so.

One interesting example is clarity on the fundamental role for a new manager. For example, in care settings, a new manager is likely focused on clinical supervision as a primary and critical role. That's so important day-to-day, but to sustain a program over time, that same manager needs to also focus on the other drivers of her program's success, especially the financial structure.

Wait, am I in the right role?

"Do I have the competencies to perform the role I'm in? Do I even like this job?" How many times have we seen a great performer promoted to a new role that doesn't rely on the competencies that made them great in the first place?

We might ask great clinicians to handle business operations or deep-thinking engineers to lead people. Sometimes people are wildly successful at adapting, but other times they might not enjoy or have competency for an expanded role. One thing is certain: even if it's the right role, we must plan and provide support to ensure an employee succeeds, which brings us to number four.

Do I have the training I need?

Having good basic competencies is only the start. Every employee needs organizational onboarding, departmental onboarding, and ongoing training and development. And if an employee is taking on a new role, success often depends on active development of a new skill set.

Sometimes training is part of a professional adjustment that is necessary for business survival, and that requires extra care to recognize employees' anxiety about change. An interesting example is the evolution in the counseling world to collaborative documentation with clients. In the past, never would a good counselor have had fingers on a keyboard during a session, and now the standard is that counselor and client work together to discuss and document the plan on the spot. Our organization made that transition with the support of outside experts who helped us plan and pace the change and provided counselor-to-counselor training to ensure all the clinical questions were addressed. Our goal was not only to provide training but to really prepare the team to lead the change. This was one element in the larger transformation of our counseling system to achieve business sustainability.

How do I know if I'm successful?

A good enterprise dashboard that centers everyone on the big picture of the key performance indicators helps keep the team focused on the big goals and tells us whether "we" are successful. But did *I* do my part? Equally important are measures for my role that support those KPIs and tell me every day, week, or month whether I'm on track to help the organization succeed. An individual performance plan with goals and metrics is a great start. Reinforcing that with continuous feedback between manager and team member gives the plan momentum.

That all sounds basic, but in organizations big and small, it's easy to let the urgent overcome the important. And how often in meetings does the problem of the moment dominate the conversation? One of the hardest things to do is stay centered on the big goals. So pull out the strategic plan often, discuss individual performance plans regularly, and measure the key performance indicators for the team and the individual. Keeping those performance indicators front and center improves the chances of success in achieving them even through all the daily distractions.

Where's my "thank-you?"

"You get a paycheck, don't you?" I am old enough to remember a time in the industrial world when your pay was your reward. Today, I think most of us recognize that people can get a paycheck anywhere. One of the reasons employees stay with you is because they feel like they're making a difference.

So make sure you notice and acknowledge the performance that aligns with your stated goals. Start with the high performers, because they're setting the pace, but equally importantly, look for alignment and progress throughout the entire team. My motto is "progress, not perfection," celebrating every successful step on the journey. Recognizing progress doesn't undermine a need for further improvement; it encourages people and keeps more of them on the path to achieving the goal. Of course, there are consequences when stated goals are not met. We can act on the low performers without letting them consume us, because the real power is in retaining the top performers and moving the middle performers to even better results.

Our team is broken.
How do we repair the damage done?

A team that isn't performing or even getting along requires a refocus on the basics. As a leader, start with yourself and make sure you're focused on all the steps above. Work together with your peers to create alignment, including learning the essential team skill of disagreeing in productive ways and moving forward together. Make sure every hard decision is made, including changes in strategy, practices, and people. Be clear in your communication and consistent in your actions. Support those pockets of the organization who really get it and are modeling the right behavior. Most importantly, remember that a reset requires patience and that success starts with the fundamentals of clarity, alignment, and an engaged team.

So how is all of this working out in my own organization? Well, I've never been more keenly aware of both the importance of leadership at every level of an organization and, at the same time, the fact that the leader herself can't achieve the results alone. We've committed to the hard work and patience it takes to engage the team, and we've properly equipped them to succeed. We built up our team problem-solving skills when things didn't go as planned. We've made sure our focus is on high- and middle-level performers and made some tough people decisions. Most importantly, the accountability we all wanted had to start at the beginning of the process as we engaged the team in defining a better, more sustainable future for the mission. As a result, the team showed up with a commitment to the goal and the ability to make a difference. We have a long journey ahead, because we're in a particularly tough business, but attrition is down 22 percent to below industry average, and financial performance is stabilizing program by program. At our organization, that means more lives saved, more people living their best lives, and the promise that we'll continue to do that for many years to come.

Values and Culture Drive Success

By Meredith Weil

I ATTRIBUTE MUCH OF my professional success to the relationships and work community I've built and nurtured through my career. It is the people in my life who help me lead successfully. I lead with the knowledge that the experiences and talents of others, when honed and focused, will create results not possible when working alone. Exceptional leaders know how and when to release control and maintain humility to accept that their method may not be the only approach to a good outcome. Great leaders give associates the opportunity to rise to the circumstances—leaders are there to guide as opposed to judge or micromanage. They allow for stumbles and celebrate progress more than perfection. Practicing extraordinary leadership is hard work, demands strong relationships, and is made better in organizations when grounded by common values.

Third Federal is a family-run, publicly traded mutual savings and loan company. Marc Stefanski became the CEO thirty-five years ago, succeeding his father and mother who started the company in 1938. Our mission is to help people achieve the dream of homeownership while creating value for our customers, associates, communities, and shareholders. Our structure is unique. We own more than 80 percent of our stock, giving us the control that allows us to deliver value to our customers, associates, and communities commensurate to what our shareholders receive. Our mission is grounded by our value system: love (a genuine concern for others), trust, commitment to excellence, treating one another with respect, and fun.

Third Federal is the first organization in my career where we purposefully use our values in our decision-making.

Running a Values-Based Organization

To operate a successful values-based organization, it is critical for leadership to believe in and exemplify the values and set the tone at the top. I work with a team of leaders who share a commitment to this driving force, so we are able to cultivate a powerful corporate culture.

Leading with the Third Federal value system keeps me and my fellow associates focused on the importance of how we interact with and treat each other and our constituents in order to deliver excellence. This is incredibly unique. Most public companies, especially banks, put profits before people. But we put people first and have experienced success not only measured by profit but also through the loyalty, commitment, and relationships our associates have with one another. Instilling our values and practicing them drives our success.

One of our practices reinforcing our values is our approach to career development. Third Federal, by design, is a very flat organization. One part of our approach to hiring makes such a difference to our corporate culture—we promote from within. By prioritizing internal candidates, with less emphasis on technical skill and more focus on understanding and the ability to manage using our values within our culture, opportunity for growth is endless. The trust and respect associates forge by experiencing new roles and forming relationships across the organization is invaluable to developing strong leaders. This approach afforded me the opportunities that prepared me for the chief operating officer role. I've held it for ten of my twenty-three years at Third Federal. One of my primary responsibilities is ensuring our values are at the core of how we operate.

Reinforcing Culture and Values

Love: During the pandemic we made the decision to award all associates with time so that if they were unable to work due to illness or quarantine, they wouldn't lose pay. Taking care of people during times of hardship is core to who we are.

Trust: The dimensions of trust include sincerity, care, competence, and reliability. With love at the core of who we are, sincerity and care are experienced consistently in the day-to-day. Prior to working at Third Federal, I'd become very accustomed to layoffs. You could predict the pattern. A quarter prior to year-end, a cost-cutting initiative was implemented. This led to restructuring and new management, and you'd either get the option to look for a new role internally or receive some sort of severance package.

Layoffs destroy trust in organizations. Third Federal has never laid people off; this is one of our cultural norms and is highlighted during conversations about our values and what they mean. As a result, our turnover is below 5 percent. Our associates can focus on working hard, especially during difficulties, instead of feeling distracted by the possibility of losing their job. Hiring decisions are thoughtfully made so we stay lean. We strive to provide each associate with an important purpose that contributes to the success of the whole.

Commitment to Excellence: When customer complaints are elevated to me, I spend time with the associate involved to improve the situation. From my position, it is easier to make exceptions. Flexibility and service recovery are critical to any organization striving for excellent customer service. Our unique approach to compensation shows a commitment to customer service. Our associates are not paid through incentives. This allows them to deliver products and services to our customers without the pressure of how it will affect their pay. Our associates are solely committed to helping their customer based on the needs of the customer.

Respect: I've found that respect is gained when given. Some behaviors I find effective for earning respect include leading by example, being present, listening to associates, and sharing ideas and opinions while reserving judgment. I presume positive intent. Trust and respect are intertwined, and when one is present, it serves to strengthen the other.

I've also found having more people with a seat at the table naturally builds confidence in associates and reinforces the mutual respect of the team. We've always used collaboration and teamwork to reach decisions.

Fun: The family atmosphere at Third Federal creates a strong source of fun in the day. The relationships I have with my fellow associates make me look forward to work. When you interact with people you genuinely care for and work together toward common purposes or goals, work is guaranteed to be fun. We also make time for celebrations and recognition and fun. We know it is important to take time to decompress daily. And even more importantly, we are all committed to having a work-life balance.

Putting Values to the Test

In the past fifteen years, we've experienced crises. But we survived, and they made us stronger. I attribute this to our values-based leadership. Challenges outside of an organization's control, whether it be from the economy, investors, regulators, customers, personal challenges, or a pandemic, can prove particularly hard on leaders. Third Federal has managed through difficult situations successfully because of the love, trust, respect, and commitment we have for one another and for the company.

During the mortgage crisis, we made the hard decision to eliminate a product offering that produced over $2 billion in customer relationships and was originated and serviced by hundreds of our associates. We eliminated the product because of losses it was producing. Also at this time, our primary regulator made it imprudent for us to pay our dividend. Our stock price dropped by half.

As a leadership team, no one cast blame for the losses we experienced. Instead, the mutual trust and respect we held for each other brought us together. We found new ways to put our associates to work, to serve our customers, and to placate our regulators. The care and concern at the forefront of our values stood at the core of our decision-making. We never contemplated layoffs. Our associates willingly worked other jobs. We launched volunteer initiatives to give people a purpose. We redesigned our product set to ensure ongoing growth. We worked with our customers to help them stay in their homes. Even though some of the risks we took prior to the crisis created losses, we had made those decisions as a team, making it impossible and unproductive to point fingers. Using our values as a guide, we focused on how to ensure our future success, and we were able to pivot the organization.

Seven years ago, my eighteen-year-old son died in a car accident. The grief and loss I felt was immeasurable. But the outpouring of love and support I felt from my Third Federal family fueled my ability to carry on.

From the executive team to branch associates, I received compassion and concern, driving me to both take care of myself and my family and know when and how to come back to work. I trusted my colleagues to make decisions in my absence so I could take the time I needed in my healing journey. I knew my reentry into work could feel strained by the empathy felt by associates in our organization, so I worked hard to put people at ease. I felt the responsibility to show leadership by not only being strong but also openly sharing my grief. When I returned, I focused on connecting with people—helping them understand I was forever changed but would lead on. I worked hard to do this on their terms. Prior to the accident, I'd led the company by listening to associates to effect change. As I reflect, I believe this process made my relationships with associates stronger and made my commitment to our values impermeable.

Prior to the pandemic, having our workforce on-site allowed us to nurture relationships and ensured that associates could disconnect from work at the end of the day. When the pandemic became a real concern, we had no choice but to change. Within several weeks, most of our nonretail workers were fully functioning from home and our retail staff had created safe working environments for both our associates and our customers on-site. The power of our shared values, especially love and excellence, was what drove our ability to pivot. Together we ensured the safety of our people and prioritized the importance of serving our customers. The pace of change we experienced has challenged our culture, but our values have remained constant. Leading associates through the pandemic proved unique because most people experienced loss—of routine, their work home, human interaction, and most tragically for some, loved ones.

When I experienced the loss of my son, people who weren't suffering were available to support me. During the pandemic, by leading with our values, we expressed our care and concern by supplementing pay, providing on-site workers extra benefits, doing virtual events, and having virtual watercooler meetings. All these efforts helped to propel our success despite the uncertain times.

Does the Success of the Organization Enable Values-Based Leadership or Does Values-Based Leadership Drive the Success?

Values can drive the success of an organization. To make this a reality, leaders must exemplify and stay committed to using company values in the day-to-day. Communicating behavior expectations creates a culture that nurtures and reinforces those values. Third Federal's collective commitment to our values drives our ongoing success through challenging times as well as seasons of stability.

JUSTNESS LESSONS LEARNED

How did leaders in this chapter foster justness?

Neeti Dewan found herself uprooted from her home, family, and friends and in a new country where she had to build her life anew. When she became an adult and entered the workforce as a professional, she again found herself among strangers who were not entirely accepting. These experiences encouraged her to commit to being a leader characterized by justness. She vowed to be open to new ideas and perspectives and to become a trusted advisor and problem-solver. And she committed herself to helping others. When she started her own businesses, she kept a few questions in the forefront:

- Does someone need an advocate?
- Would a word of encouragement and acknowledgment make a difference in someone's work life?
- Is someone not getting credit?
- Who is not invited to the table but should be?

Neeti uses these questions to guide actions. She strives to apply her principles and chooses to be an advocate instead of someone standing on the sidelines.

When **Elaine Russell Reolfi** became CEO of a behavioral health organization, she entered an underperforming nonprofit that had a "smart and passionate team brimming with frustration." The team believed that accountability was needed to improve effectiveness.

Accountability is often prescriptive and measured. While Elaine implemented individual and team performance plans, she began the process of reversing poor performance by aligning team members around purpose and values. She asked, "What impact are we trying to make on the world over time?" She also defined values that would guide behaviors between individuals.

These fundamental guideposts became a rubric for accountability, but instead of employees being accountable to a supervisor, employees became accountable to themselves and to each other. Individuals, therefore, aspired to fulfill commitments of care toward each other and the mission of the organization.

Elaine also shows justness through her motto of "progress, not perfection," encouraging team members to use good judgment and act even if they are unsure of the outcome. Hence, she provides team members with opportunities to grow, develop, and test skills.

Under **Meredith Weil**'s leadership as COO at Third Federal Savings & Loan, justness is found at the individual, team, and organizational levels.

At the individual level, Meredith's just leadership is demonstrated through interactions with employees. She assumes positive intent when listening to ideas, concerns, and opinions. Notably, after suffering a tragic loss, she shared her grief but also showed strength and a promise to continue to lead. In this way, she led by example showing others how to be resilient under the most painful circumstances. This is a form of justness, as it demonstrates an ethic of care. Weil was concerned that the employees would not know how to express their empathy and intercepted their discomfort through openness.

At the team level, Meredith shows justness by making many decisions collaboratively and by valuing fun. Fun is one of five principles that guide the organization and is expressed through celebrations, recognition, and daily interactions that express friendship and caring.

At the organizational level, Meredith demonstrates justness through policies of hiring from within and caring for employees during crises. Her organization offers employees opportunities to work in various positions throughout the bank, helping them develop new skills and relationships that will enable them to rise within the ranks of the bank. Her organization's policies have also placed employees' needs above the organization's needs while simultaneously working to make changes to ensure the organization's long-term success. During the national mortgage crisis, Third Federal eliminated a product producing $2 billion because it was losing money. However, there were no layoffs, the bank made sure that customers could stay in their homes, and they replaced the product with a better version. Additionally, during the pandemic, employees did not lose pay if they were ill or quarantined, and the bank created programs to keep employees engaged while working remotely.

In Sum

The narratives in this chapter illustrate how to demonstrate justness in the workplace. These practices include:

- Shape policies to elevate employees and care for their well-being.
- Develop trusting relationships that indicate personal needs will be balanced with organizational needs.
- Be nonjudgmental when listening to ideas.
- Acknowledge and celebrate positive contributions.

- Empower others.
- Show employees that the organization cares about managing stress.

Reflective Questions

1. How do you identify diverse strengths amongst your employees to create more effective teams?
2. How do you get to know your team and what they can contribute?
3. Imagine ways in which you can emphasize collaborative culture versus competitive culture.
4. How do you cultivate trust between you as a leader and your employees?
5. How does justness contribute to retention, engagement, and intrinsic motivation?
6. How do you focus beyond being task- and transaction oriented to developing transformational opportunities for employees and the organization?
7. How do you make sure that there is transparency in your organization so that employees feel involved and participate in making decisions?
8. How are you approaching other members of your organization with positive intent?
9. What are the ways that you make sure to recognize, value, and celebrate the strengths of employees, and how does that contribute toward justness?

CHAPTER 8

Intrinsic Motivation: Business Is Personal

CHAPTER 1 DESCRIBES THIS Core Differentiator, intrinsic motivation, as the emotional drive to go above and beyond one's narrow self-interest for mutually rewarding and beneficial outcomes within a community or organization. The leader creates an environment in which the employee feels connected and the work is personal. This results in an employee being more engaged and productive. Specifically, they are more willing to come to the aid of their colleagues, protect the relationship with customers, and overall be more conscientious. When a leader exhibits intrinsic motivation, it makes the culture flourish.

THE CORE DIFFERENTIATORS

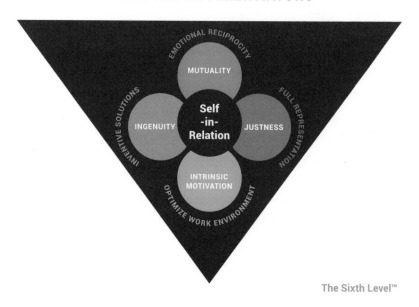

The Sixth Level™

Rewriting the Rules of a Successful Acquisition

By Rachel Wallis Andreasson

AT OUR RECENT BOARD meeting, our CFO reported another record-breaking financial month, a result of the largest acquisition in our company's history, purchased five years earlier. A sense of gratitude washed over me. I said a silent thank-you to my dad, the founder of our company and a servant leader who taught me the importance of building relationships in business.

Putting the strategic pieces in place to make this latest investment happen resulted from relationships I'd formed. Just as Dad had spearheaded the acquisition that brought me to work at the family business thirty years before, I knew I was following his lead. As I listened to the CFO's report, I felt validated knowing this procurement was accomplishing what I'd known it could. I paused, sensing my deceased father's pride and realizing that my work honored his legacy. The CFO's report assured me that the stage was now set for long-term viability. It affirmed my belief that bringing in the third generation was the right path for the future. I smiled to myself, reflecting on the unlikely nature of this acquisition.

The work to undertake the asset purchase started at an annual leadership retreat. The topic was growth, and the strategy was acquisitions. A competitor's name came up as a possible target, but our board felt it was not possible. I took that as a challenge. I was responsible for the convenience store division that would gain from the assets if we closed on this investment, so I quietly opposed the board's sentiments. I was certain this acquisition would catapult our company's growth, as it made sense culturally, geographically, and financially. And I believed attaining the business was possible if approached with care.

In my MBA program, I learned the chief reason 70 to 90 percent of acquisitions fail is due to a lack of integration. From my father, I also learned what worked and what did not work when integrating acquired companies. I visualized the steps it would take to build a relationship with our competitor and the future synergies that would result if I succeeded. Then I got to work.

When I was a young child, I attended conventions with my parents and sat at the table with the founders of the company we wanted to purchase. Many years after I joined our company, I became acquainted with their son, and he and I served on our state association board. At the time, the son was the president of the association, and when his term ended, I became the first female president. Those personal relationships were important.

As a first step in developing a deeper connection, I invited him to breakfast. We discussed what it is like to be a part of a family business and the parallels of our organizations. I knew I had to take a step forward in building trust and showing vulnerability. I asked him to allow our company to be a customer of their commissary. After months of negotiation, we moved all our commissary business to their facility.

Our arrangement proved successful. When I approached the son about other possibilities, I learned their family had hired an investment banker to sell their assets. I asked if we could have a seat at the negotiation table. He expressed concern that our family business could not stand up to the offers of major national chains like Circle K, but I squelched his concerns by giving him specific examples of our financial wherewithal. I knew, however, that the true heart of the matter was taking care of their employees. I quickly laid out specifics on how their team would be cared for within our organization. We ended the conversation with his commitment to send me a confidentiality agreement.

Over the next five months, our acquisition team progressed in full force. Our CFO did the financial modeling and worked to secure the necessary financing. Our team had a process in place from previous investments and worked diligently on the details of integrating people, systems, and technology. Whenever we felt we were losing traction, the son and I would talk, getting my company back into motion. The day finally came when we signed the letter of intent. We were now the sole buyer.

The confidentiality agreement remained in force, but in due time, the son called to say his employees sensed something was changing. We had to release a statement immediately. That became our first unifying moment. It signaled our need to turn attention toward integrating the workforces—toward the people.

I knew what a shock it would be if our employees ever found out we were selling, and I empathized with their employees' feelings. We had to come out of the gate strong and build trust. This meant the seller and I needed to agree upon statements each company would issue and share. I needed to get to work with his team and pull some town hall meetings together. We scheduled fourteen meetings six weeks before we closed. The founder kicked off each meeting by explaining why their family chose to sell, and I explained what was it in for employees if they stayed. I assured them that no one would lose tenure. If they had worked for the seller for ten years, we would credit them for ten years with our company. I answered questions as our human resources team handed out employee packets for people to complete. On the day we closed, they would be formally hired and on our payroll. I committed to no policy or procedure changes for ninety days so we could figure out how to integrate the best of both companies. Lastly, I confirmed that if employees stayed for the full ninety days to give us a try, they would receive a retention bonus.

My favorite part of the town hall meetings was when the founder introduced me to his team. He called out specific store sales and recognized individual team members' accomplishments. It made me realize how much he cared about his employees and his resolve that employees felt valued. I was eager to continue his leadership practices.

I also enjoyed celebratory drinks after completing the three to four town hall meetings with the founder, his management team, and my team. We talked about the acquisition process, and he shared stories about the company's history. This generational knowledge provided key insights into what made his company successful and what made his employees feel respected.

The collaboration of our two organizations was energizing, but one moment in particular felt deeply moving for me. After the final town hall meeting, the founder pulled me aside and asked, "Do you know why we sold to you even though we had better offers from bigger companies?"

I shook my head no.

He looked at me and said simply, "I knew you would take care of my people."

That statement increased my determination. I knew we got a seat at the table because we were a person-focused company. But after hearing his heart, I was even more committed to not let him or his team down.

After the initial efforts to integrate our companies were completed, I continued to build trust and unity by circulating a Friday email. This email began with a personal reflection that not only conveyed my beliefs but also exposed my vulnerability. I wanted to send the message that it was okay for the team to do the same. The email offered an opportunity to maintain transparency. I shared what we were doing behind the scenes to integrate the two organizations and reported on what other divisions within our organizations were doing. I concluded the email with a "Friday Funny," honoring their founder, who always started the town hall meetings with a few jokes. This email helped promote a vision of moving forward as one team. Like clockwork, each Friday around 5:00 a.m., the email was sent to all 1,100 team members. But the town hall meetings and Friday emails were only part of our strategies to unite our companies.

We also paired managers from each company in a sort of "buddy system." The "buddies" exchanged information and relied on each other to help navigate the new environment. I also hired a certified coach to help facilitate the "best of both." Each company selected eight managers to work together on the ninety-day team. The goal was to leverage the strengths from each side and come together with a plan to make us a stronger team and more powerful organization.

Our companies had a lot to learn from each other even though we shared many of the same operational characteristics. For example, their company had created a strong brand called *Dirt Cheap* that resonated with customers and team members as light and fun. Our company had organizational structures such as the balanced scorecard, which made key performance indicators clear. Sharing these operational strategies made the acquisition smoother and brought the team members on board more quickly. We also collaborated on issues such as monthly bonus programs, new uniforms after the first ninety days, how to streamline food products under one label, personal appearance policy, and how to onboard new hires. Each company was accustomed to different practices, but every single manager went above and beyond for the greater good and presented their recommendations on how to move forward together.

The best example highlighting the success of the "best of both" occurred at the group's last meeting. The facilitator suggested we all stand in a circle with one person in the middle. That person's only job was to not speak and instead look in the eyes of each person in the outer circle. When their eyes met, the person on the outside shared a quality about the person in the middle that they admired.

The first person who made eye contact started. "You were calm under pressure during the presentation."

"You are great at explaining difficult concepts," said the next.

"I love your sense of humor," said the third.

"I have worked with you for ten years but never really knew you, and I am so glad I do now."

I could literally see the strong bond growing as it was created, and it filled my heart.

Reflecting on the priorities that made the integration unique is something I enjoy. Turning my attention back to the board meeting, I listened as our CFO detailed our historical financial progress and our nonfamily CEO outlined expansion plans for our brands. This included *Dirt Cheap*, the brand we purchased five years ago. We'd exceeded our expectations in all categories. It was a massive victory I attributed to my dad, the previous owner of the business we'd acquired, and the willingness of the next-generation leaders brought together from two different companies to lead with heart. I felt proud knowing we'd beaten the odds. I believe listening to our employees and conscientiously addressing their material and emotional needs made our acquisition a success and helped us rewrite the rules for future investments.

Releasing the Power of Purpose

By Jodi Berg

I HAD THE OPPORTUNITY to catapult our fourth-generation family business, Vitamix, from a beloved niche product to a world-renowned, iconic brand. We are credited for redefining the blender category and permanently altering food preparation in the consumer and food service industries. In a few short years, we navigated hyper growth at all levels of our manufacturing process, exceeded customer expectations, tripled our footprint and workforce, and expanded into multiple countries. We became a powerhouse in the health and wellness space centered around whole food. Awards for our products, customer service, wellness programs, entrepreneurial spirit, and most significantly, high-performing, purpose-driven culture symbolize the impact we've had. Here is our story.

Multiple perspectives abound on facilitating change. I break it into two key phases: an opportunity and a means to make it happen. For me the path to our future was crystal clear. The world was changing rapidly, and I saw an opportunity for Vitamix to be a key player in permanently changing the way people understood the role of food in our health. The challenge was making it happen.

Forging the Means to Make It Happen

Having a vision or opportunity is nothing without a means to get there. Being a small company in a field of very large competitors, we needed to act quickly, accurately, and purposefully, transforming the entire organization and industry without waking the sleeping giants. Knowing no one person or top leadership team could do this alone, I intuitively knew we needed to unleash the individual and collective motivations of our entire workforce. The average level of engagement of employees in the US is close to 30 percent, and we needed significantly more than that to succeed.

Spoiler alert: our engagement levels flew off the charts. The result was more powerful than I could have dreamed or imagined.

Why? I knew traditional leadership practices were not sufficient. So I used my gut. I reflected on times when I was so motivated, focused, and driven that nothing would stop me from succeeding. I realized that when the purpose and/or goal is personal, it is as if I acquire superpowers and I overcome any obstacle in the way. I set out to create a culture that released this same passion, commitment, and tenacity in others. By making their role and our vision personal to every employee, we met their highest level of Maslow's hierarchy of needs, self-actualization, in a way that drove organizational performance.

This approach works because clarity of purpose creates a laser focus on the endgame. Making that purpose personal generates agility and resolve to conquer adversity. However, creating a culture in which the purpose is not only personal but shared with others is when the true magic happens. To understand this, reflect on a time when you set out to achieve something that was personally meaningful to you. A time when nothing could stop you from accomplishing that thing because it truly mattered. Now imagine igniting and harnessing this internal motivation in every one of your employees!

Debunking Leadership Myths

We were successful in creating a culture that harnesses internal motivation, creating and navigating hyper growth and becoming an iconic brand, because we debunked several traditional leadership assumptions.

Assumption number one: we have been taught that external incentives designed to help employees feel good, such as improving employee recognition programs, providing flexibility, having celebrations, and the like, are motivating. Books about improving company culture are filled with this message.

External motivation techniques, either a carrot or a stick, have been around for a while with no evidence that they have a tangible or sustainable impact on engagement. Motivation is an internal process or condition. It can either be developed by the environment (extrinsic) or by oneself (intrinsic). Extrinsic motivation comes from external stimulation and drives the desire to perform for a reward or to avoid punishment. Intrinsic motivation, both more effective and more sustainable, comes from within, igniting personal satisfaction by performing an activity.

While earning a PhD in management and designing sustainable systems, and while researching leadership, I found that motivation is even greater when there is a personal connection to a greater purpose. If a company vision or purpose is meaningful, a deep, almost spiritual commitment and desire to make the world a better place through one's organization is born.

To be authentic, company statements such as shared values, purpose, or mission must come from within the hearts and souls of everyone involved. At Vitamix, we used appreciative inquiry to expeditiously engage all stakeholder groups—employees, customers, suppliers, owners, and the community—in a process to identify the values we already shared and craft our vision and mission statements. Next, leadership adopted the cultural elements developed by these groups and became stewards of our shared culture. We took it to a completely different level by purposefully helping employees identify their personal purpose and how this, our company purpose, and their job were symbiotically connected. Consequently, by fulfilling their role at Vitamix, they were living with their personal purpose front and center while driving company performance.

An example of the value of this approach is reflected in one employee's touching response to a customer testimonial that I shared with our production team. Carmen was brought to tears. When I was comforting her later, she explained that she realized her hands may have built the unit that had transformed that child's life. Carmen's purpose in life was to make people's lives better. She said she would never build another machine without recognizing that lives can and will be changed because of what she was doing.

My purpose in life is to help people find their wings and give them a chance to fly. By doing this every day with my fellow employees, customers, and other stakeholders, I was able to advance our company purpose and drive performance.

Assumption number two: culture is static and difficult to change.

A company culture is a set of values, beliefs, and attitudes. As the people within an organization and situations change, the culture adjusts. So culture is always in motion and will evolve either purposefully or by default. If we want to use culture as a powerful tool to release engagement, commitment, and motivation, we need to evolve it intentionally.

The elements of our new shared culture became a part of everything we said and did. It was printed not only on our walls but on a card that every one of us carried. We talked about it in meetings, referred to it in communications, and made decisions individually and collectively after reflecting and discussing relevant aspects of our culture.

Our culture was introduced in the interview process, elaborated on in orientation, and used in performance conversations. Leaders were charged the critical role of creating and maintaining a place where employees witnessed an uncompromising commitment to this culture. Additionally, to ensure our culture was sustainable, we hired new employees who already shared our values and were passionate about our purpose. This practice had the added advantage that new employees immediately felt at home with their fellow employees and quickly felt secure in contributing.

The more employees saw the commitment by leadership to ensure our culture—*their* culture—was not going to be compromised, the faster change happened.

The strength of our new culture was demonstrated when we expanded so rapidly, we outgrew our headquarters. We needed another facility, and there was concern that our culture would not survive the geographical split. To our delight, the new facility was up and running in record time, and the culture endured, just as powerful as ever.

Assumption number three: leaders are the most effective at making the culture and work environment better.

Traditional leadership encourages leaders to seek input when developing a culture. This explicitly sends the message that although leadership appreciates the perspective of employees, the "powers that be" will ultimately make the decision. We flipped this command-and-control mindset on its head.

At Vitamix, instead of asking employees how leadership can make things better, we had open conversations, leaving all titles at the door, about how we could collaborate and improve our shared culture.

An example of this phenomenon was at the onset of COVID. We set our priorities together, with the prime concern being employee safety followed by business sustainability. Each work team was given the authority to do whatever they felt they needed. Leadership did not decide what they needed; we shared the parameters, let them decide, then stepped into a stewardship role to help them make it happen.

We collectively decided we wanted our fellow employees to feel safe. Our on-site employees voiced concern that their families needed reassurance that their loved ones working in our facilities were safe. In response, our operations department held an art contest in which their children created posters to remind their parents how to stay safe at work. The operations team created large versions of these posters and hung them all around the facility.

There Are Two Sides to Releasing the Power of Intrinsic Motivation

On one hand, people need to truly believe they are safe and supported in making decisions and choices they believe will achieve the shared purpose; this is critical. Conversely, the company needs to feel safe when releasing control and decision-making authority. This is possible when a shared culture is authentically created and when the mechanisms are in place to ensure it is symbiotic, or mutually beneficial, to both the employees and the organization. Achieving both objectives is necessary to create a culture that authentically recognizes employees are people with personal needs *and* drives company performance.

The concept of feeling secure is worth some discussion. When we feel safe, we are more willing to take healthy risks. For example, knowing there is a safety net makes all the difference to a trapeze artist. Employees take risks when they know their company supports them and is willing to catch them if they fall or fail.

At Vitamix we felt safe transferring the power from a small subset of leadership to the collective group of employees because our culture was developed by those employees. The employees had helped develop policies and structures such as hiring, recognition, and removal to support the symbiotic alignment between themselves and the company. Why? Because this was their culture, and the employees did not want their culture compromised!

It worked like a dream. It was deeply rewarding to stand up in front of a group and authentically credit the amazing people who worked for and with Vitamix, knowing that it was our shared creation and commitment. Specifically, it was the harnessing of intrinsic motivation, released individually, that made it happen. We did not simply talk about empowerment—we lived it. We found that empowering employees to create and therefore own the culture far outweighed the risk. The performance that resulted and being a part of a vibrant and connected culture are their own rewards.

Over the years, my company and I have received a plethora of accolades. But my favorite by far is when I was voted "Most Likeable CEO in Cleveland." That label is not one I earned alone—it took a team of amazing individuals, people who saw the opportunity and who joined forces *with* me, to make it happen.

Sweet Memories Can Recreate Success

By Stephanie Stuckey, CEO of Stuckey's

WHEN I WAS A little girl, my grandfather, W.S. Stuckey, often gave me and his other grandchildren Stuckey's pecan log rolls as a treat. Those iconic candies, a recipe perfected by my grandmother in 1937, were a huge part of the amazing journey of his namesake stores. My grandfather had spent his entire life building Stuckey's from its humble roots as a roadside stand to a recognizable name with 350 stores dotting the highways of America. Stuckey's, the first roadside retail chain in the country, was synonymous with the experience of road-tripping and finding hidden gems in the small towns along the way.

I can still remember tearing open the candy's wrapper, inhaling the sweet, syrupy scent of the pralines, and taking a bite of the chewy pecan-nougat goodness while catching just a hint of maraschino cherry (my grandmother's secret ingredient). I have hundreds of memories wrapped around that candy bar, which to me still tastes like the best of my childhood.

My grandfather sold the chain before I was born, but he often talked fondly about the millions of travelers who stopped by one of his stores for a respite from their road trip. He died in 1977, just before the newest owners of the chain began slowly shuttering the stores. By the time I had an opportunity to buy back the company, 80 percent of the stores he had opened were gone. I had one mission—to honor my grandfather's legacy by turning Stuckey's around.

I walked into a mess. The company was six figures in debt, the stores were a disaster, and profits were minimal. The magic my grandfather had brought to the brand was gone. The famous pecan log roll was just one more item on the crowded shelves. I thought of something my grandfather had written in his papers: "Every traveler [I met] was a friend." I wondered how I could ever possibly evoke that spirit in Stuckey's again.

I reflected on my many memories wrapped up in those candy bars, and I knew that if I could bring that same sense of anticipation and warmth to the stores, customers, and employees, I would have the recipe for reviving Stuckey's. However, as I looked at the balance sheet, I realized that I was going to have to release one key ingredient if we were going to make this work—the stores.

For decades, the blue-roofed Stuckey's stores were seen as a place where weary travelers could pull over for gas refills, clean restrooms, delicious snacks, and fun souvenirs. The stores that were left had been licensed to independent owners who were only generating 10 percent of our revenue. I had to make the hard, emotional decision to stop focusing on brick-and-mortar and find another way to rebuild the brand.

I decided to look back in order to look forward, even though I faced opposition from some members of our management team who wanted to keep operating the way we always had. The numbers didn't lie. The profit-makers were the pecan log rolls, other unique candies, and nut sales, just as they had been when my grandfather started in the 1930s.

In his first year in business selling Georgia pecans, my grandfather made $4,500, a small fortune then. He thought candy would make a great add-on, so he asked my grandmother Ethel to create a pecan log roll. Every single day, she and her sisters would make the candies in her kitchen and then walk the two miles from her house to Grandpa's roadside stand, a glorified lean-to he'd set up along Route 23 in Hilliard, Georgia. That addition of candy transformed Stuckey's future and my grandparents' lives. Going back to those roots seemed to be the smartest financial path, but we had a lot of obstacles to overcome in shifting our focus to retail manufacturing.

World War II had shut my grandfather down for several years, as rationing and supplies made it impossible to keep selling candy. But when the war was over, he received a government grant to fund his manufacturing operation. Now, eighty years later, I applied for pandemic relief funds from the government and used those to find a location in rural Georgia where I could rebuild our manufacturing division.

My grandfather's original plant had long ago been shuttered, but I found another plant two hours away that was making the exact same kind of candy we were. Ironically, they were one of the pecan suppliers for my grandfather when he first started out in the 1930s. I brought on two partners and bought the plant, and we got to work producing pecan rolls and other treats.

Our leadership team spent a few days hammering out the strategy that would provide us a path forward. We had some heated discussions because everyone in the room felt passionate about Stuckey's, but we were finally able to nail down our purpose. Whether you're visiting a branded Stuckey's store or walking down the aisle of your local grocery store, we want Stuckey's products to make people feel special and like they're your friends.

We worried whether people would remember the Stuckey's brand and embrace it as they had before. Would our marketing evoke those feelings of camaraderie and care? Could we deliver that same sense of a roadside treat that the stores once had? I had faced tough battles all my life, both as an attorney and as a member of the Georgia legislature, but this time, the challenge was personal. I didn't want to let my late grandfather down or allow my family name to become a sidenote in history.

We rebranded our website and marketing materials to capture the fun anticipation that comes with opening your favorite candy bar. Our goal was to make sure that sense of intrinsic motivation was baked into every Stuckey's experience, both for the customers and the team members. With customers, if their activity—like opening a delicious candy bar—evokes feelings of joy, then they will feel a sense of intrinsic motivation.[1]

As we worked through the leadership transition, we made it a priority to ask the hard questions and to listen to our people's responses. If you wait until the employee exit interview, it's too late. Today, I'm continually inviting those conversations and asking people, "How can I make your job better?" That internal return on your investment of time or money is also crucial in employee retention.[2] People like to feel that the company they work for cares about them and the work they do. In fact, a recent LinkedIn survey found that 71 percent of Americans want to work for a company that matches their values.[3]

A year ago, I had a conversation with Dan Cathy, former CEO of Chick-fil-A. I was still new at the helm of Stuckey's, nervous about whether I would be able to turn things around and make Stuckey's profitable again. Cathy asked me to nail down my purpose because that would be the root of our turnaround.

After that conversation, I realized it wasn't just about the purpose of Stuckey's—it was also about my purpose as a CEO. What change did I want to bring to the table? How could I transform the company culture and the Stuckey's experience? At first, I didn't have those answers. I'd spent three decades as an environmental attorney. When I first started as CEO, I couldn't read a balance sheet and had no idea how to run a company. But as I flipped through my grandfather's papers, I realized he had already set the path—by treating every traveler like a friend.

I decided to handle my team with the same welcoming spirit of generosity I'd learned from my grandfather. I opened the table to discussions and opinions and listened carefully to each person's input. I wanted my team to feel like I cared about them as people and about their ideas for the company. That approach extended beyond the corporate office—I also wanted every person who was involved with Stuckey's, from vendors to retailers, to feel that same sense of friendship when they worked with us.

There were many days when I'd put on a hairnet and work the line with the employees. I wanted to learn as much as I could about the process and show the team that I was in it with them. Reviving the brand meant a lot to me, which meant the people who were part of that revival also meant a lot. I think working the line with the employees sent a strong message of "We're in this together."

I gave every team member my phone number and made sure to be on call 24-7. I talked to every person who had a question or a concern, because I knew that this would only work if we all worked together. It was scary, without a doubt. The prospect of turning around a company that was six figures in debt was daunting. It's very rare for a family to lose their company and then get it back, and even rarer to make the second iteration a success.

I'm proud to say we've paid homage to the nostalgic aspect of our brand, essentially reimagining and repackaging the history so many people still remember. We took a brand that was hearing its death knell and revived it by being brave enough to let go of the brick-and-mortar and embrace a new life in consumer packaged goods. The battle isn't over. We're still on our comeback journey, but it's an adventure that means as much to me as it did to my grandfather.

The intrinsic motivation for me comes when I open one of those wrappers and take a bite of my grandmother's famous pecan candy. In my mind, I hear my grandfather telling me that he's proud of the job I have done and that this is just the first of many sweet moments in the comeback story of the beloved Stuckey's brand.

INTRINSIC MOTIVATION
LESSONS LEARNED

How did leaders in this chapter foster intrinsic motivation?

When **Rachel Wallis Andreasson** closed a monumental merger agreement, she was immediately confronted with the daunting task of uniting two companies, including their separate corporate cultures. Policies stimulating intrinsic motivation helped her succeed in this high-risk task. She set up fourteen town hall meetings in quick succession to inform stakeholders of the merger and what it will mean for them corporately and individually. She created a "buddy system" and brought in a coach to promote relationships between teams and individuals. She also instituted a Friday email to keep employees informed and to inject unifying humor into the system. All these policies demonstrated her care in responding to employees' concerns and Rachel's interest in helping employees do their best. In turn, the policies and practices generated a sense of belonging and a desire to contribute to the greater good. Employees were intrinsically motivated to make the merger successful.

Cultivating intrinsic motivation helped **Jodi Berg** evoke her employees' superpowers as she seized on a pivotal opportunity with a tight time frame. While conscious of the time press, Jodi took the time to gather employees in groups to discuss the purpose of Vitamix and the values they would like to see Vitamix embrace. She crafted a company vision statement from their input and then asked employees to discuss how they connected individually to the vision statement. She found that the more employees connected to the vision statement, the more they were committed to corporate goals. Her focus on a higher purpose inspired employees and gave meaning to their work, thus generating intrinsic motivation. Consequently, Vitamix succeeded in growing 400 percent.

Stephanie Stuckey activated intrinsic motivation by reviving her family business, Stuckey's, around the passion and values of her grandfather, a well-known and respected figure in the community and across the nation. She also replicated his humility and care for employees by seeking their input and donning a hairnet to join them on the manufacturing front line. Furthermore, Stephanie offered her phone number to employees with an invitation to call her anytime. By building a community around her grandmother's pecan log, she and her dedicated employees overcame the odds in revivifying her family's business. Her caring mindset toward employees and her desire to revive a national symbol stirred a sense of meaning in employees who became intrinsically motivated.

In Sum

The narratives in this chapter illustrate how to put the concept of intrinsic motivation into practice, which includes:

- Offering town hall or group meetings to give employees the opportunity to share, listen, and implement improvements.

- Developing a statement of purpose and values (known as a vision statement) based on input from management and other employees.
- Asking employees and listening as they explain how they connect with the mission and/or vision statement and live out these statements.
- Engaging employees to improve processes and practices.
- Engaging employees in the leader's passion for the organization.
- Engaging with employees at all levels.

Reflective Questions

1. Do you feel engaged and willing to go above and beyond at work?
2. When was a time you felt that way, and why?
3. When have you not felt that way, and why?
4. How does your own sense of being intrinsically motivated translate to your team so they also feel intrinsically motivated?
5. What can you do as a leader to create an environment where employees feel personally connected to the organization's success?

The Sixth Level Advantage

FIGURE 6. THE X-FACTOR: SIXTH LEVEL LEADERSHIP

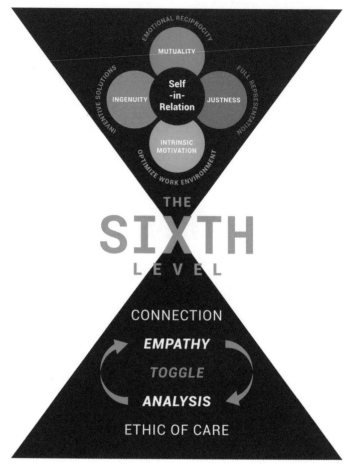

The Sixth Level™

WE CALL FIGURE 6 The X-Factor because it is the culmination of the intersection of the four core differentiators and the mental process we refer to as toggling. Point "X" is the inflection point of Sixth Level leadership and activates Self-in-Relation. The Sixth Level advantage capitalizes the power of women's psychology for sustainable leadership.

CHAPTER 9

A New Leadership Model that Produces Better Outcomes

"We've realized that women can do what men can do.
The next leap?
Realizing that men can do what women can do."
—Gloria Steinem

A New Model of Leadership

The lessons and stories of Sixth Level leadership throughout this book demonstrates we are gaining momentum as we enter a new era, we can elevate out of patriarchy towards a society based on the ethic of care.

As organizations and companies across the country and around the world dedicate themselves to the principles of Self-in-Relation, as they place mutuality, ingenuity, justness, and intrinsic motivation at the center of their corporate culture, we will all be richer and more fulfilled.

But implementing Sixth Level leadership is not easy, it is a commitment to a new mindset. It involves creating a new culture within an organization, where the four Core Differentiators of mutuality, ingenuity, justness, and intrinsic motivation are unequivocally embraced, practiced, modeled, valued, and respected. This must be a culture that yields a higher level of engagement where team members are heard, involved, respected, and intrinsically motivated to work hard for the good of the entire organization and all the individuals within it. This movement will depend on courageous leaders embracing a new paradigm—and leaving the old one behind.

How exactly do you do that? How do you exercise Sixth Level leadership—and how do you replace command and control with Self-in-Relation?

There is no silver bullet, and just when you feel like things are headed in the right direction, there is invariably a setback. Consider this example from Rachel Wallis Andreasson:

> I began a new career as the executive director of a religious not-for-profit and loved my job. When I started, there were a few deep-rooted issues affecting the staff and morale. Decisions were not being made, information was not accessible or offered in a transparent way, and there was a deep divide between the board and the staff. Over the next two and a half years, I worked hard to change that culture and mindset. We were making good progress, implementing sustainable systems that would live beyond any one person.
>
> Then COVID hit our community hard. We were the first organization in St. Louis to be on local and national news for one of our beloved teachers being hospitalized. The school shut down, and we were able to continue to pay our teachers due to the payroll protection program, and we capitalized on this time to do a major renovation while there were no students or teachers in the building. Needless to say, the year was exhausting.
>
> The following April, as we were just starting to crawl our way out, we were invited to participate in a nationwide engagement

survey. To the best of anyone's knowledge, a survey of the staff had never been done before. I thought everything was fine. The results were alarming! As a leader, you cannot help but feel a sense of responsibility for terrible results. The top concerns were around well-being, diversity, equity, inclusion, and collaboration. My first instinct was to step in and institute a raft of changes I felt would help fix the situation. However, our communications director expressed a desire to step up and take a lead role in repairing the culture, and even though it was hard to let go at first, in the end, it turned out to be a great decision. The end result is that we worked to put the right people in the right positions, we elevated transparency and sharing of information, and we have done many things to build a bridge between the board and staff.

When a leader experiences a setback, which there will be, a Sixth Level leader will pivot and recover.

How Do You Create a New Culture?

Creating a culture involves articulating a certain set of values, sharing those values with the community, listening to the input and concerns of the team, modeling those values yourself, and supporting those values in others. Creating a new culture often means replacing the old culture. Moving out of a paradigm is challenging. It means going against the grain, interrupting destructive patterns of behavior, and asking a workforce stuck in old patterns ("We have always done it this way") and entangled in relationship disappointments to embrace a new way.

New organizational culture takes months and years to develop and take hold. It requires dedication and consistency, flexibility and humility, and the ability to toggle between the empathetic and analytical[1]—behaviors that many leaders find difficult to consistently practice. But remember: organizational systems based on Self-in-Relation have better outcomes for all. Leaders who embrace The Sixth Level bust the myth that profits and growth cannot occur simultaneously with mutuality, inclusion, and justness. Rather, The Sixth Level produces all these benefits, leading to the ultimate goal: sustainability.

Get Comfortable with the Uncomfortable

Sixth Level leadership requires leaders to stretch beyond the familiar into areas that can feel very uncomfortable. Ingenuity is the Core Differentiator that elevates problem-solving and moves leaders toward better resolutions.

As we have seen throughout this book, The Sixth Level model defines ingenuity as a complex human quality that delivers inventive solutions for communities while addressing the needs of individuals. By bridging community and individual needs, promoting collaboration, and embracing inclusive decision-making, ingenuity propels an organization forward and has the power to create a more inclusive, equitable, and thriving world for all.

Ingenuity encompasses creative problem-solving, critical thinking, adaptability, resourcefulness, and the ethic of care.[2] This complexity allows leaders to navigate challenges and arrive at innovative solutions that address the diverse needs and interests of individuals in the service of a unified community.

This kind of complex decision-making, a process that includes building relationships and nurturing connections, can be messy. It's much neater (and faster) to sit in your office, study the information, evaluate the research, and come to a decision by yourself.

Another example from Rachel Wallis Andreasson happened in one of her organizations, as she explains:

> We had a history of acquisitions. And we had an individual leading a division that was doing multiple acquisitions who decided he didn't need to use an acquisition team for a particular deal. He just ran solo with a select few from his own team. This exclusion of support divisions led to key issues not being discovered in the due diligence phase, which then catapulted after the closing date. When we asked the CEO if we could create a team, the decision was no. They had it under control. In the end, this acquisition was a failure. We lost key sales personnel and customers. The integration took longer than any other acquisition, and the profitability was dismal. It took us years to turn this around simply because two leaders operated in a vacuum and missed the viewpoint of integrating the culture, the people, and the systems. The process was unsustainable.

Sustainability requires ingenuity. As a leader, you can promote ingenuity by creating inclusive spaces where diverse voices are heard, valued, and incorporated into the problem-solving process. In its simplest form, that means inviting more people to the table from a variety of backgrounds, levels of seniority, and experiences. Make your meeting table a place of lively variety and inclusion. The team needs to be diverse, and the leader needs to ensure everyone feels encouraged and empowered to contribute.

When a leader has a complex problem to solve, you need to be transparent in the communication of what the complex problem is. Circulate ideas in advance. Make sure you think broadly about who you're going to include on your team.

You also must be willing to listen. Don't rush to judgment—refuse to fall victim to your own ego and surround yourself with people who keep you in check. Focus on finding the best solution, not trying to convince everyone to adopt yours.

Ultimately leaders must make decisions. Many decisions cannot and should not be made by majority vote, because most members of an organization do not have the global perspective of the entire company, which the leader must have. Sixth Level leaders do not abdicate their decision-making role, but they approach decision-making in a totally new way through a process that enables them to make complex decisions that benefit the individuals, the team, and the organization.

Pillars of Justness Support
Sustainable Corporate Cultures

Sixth Level leaders are insistent about ensuring justness within their organizations—starting with the decision-making process but not ending there. Inclusion and respect for others are not just key elements of mutuality and ingenuity; they are pillars of the entire culture of Sixth Level organizations. So how do you promote and protect justness within your organization? First, you must actively look for avenues that allow input from multiple stakeholders and a variety of voices. Be quick to give public credit for accomplishments and ideas, and never take credit for someone else's work. At the same time, do not punish risk-taking or even failure, but encourage the entire team to learn from mistakes.

Again, this doesn't mean performance doesn't matter. Of course, if an employee consistently fails to meet goals or is simply unable to perform a job, a leader must make the tough decision to either reassign them or relieve them of duty. Some organizations have a culture to hire fast and fire fast, where the leader is impulsive and the well-being of the individual and the organization is not holistically considered. The key is to ensure that all members of the team are given equal opportunity to participate, to learn, to grow, to be involved as much as practical, and to succeed. A level playing field, where each employee feels a sense of opportunity and respect, creates a just community.

One of the trickiest areas is personnel, Rachel Wallis Andreasson gives us an example:

> One of the most difficult things I have had to do as an executive is terminating long-term employees. One of the hardest occurred in 2015 when the board mandated that I fire a division head before I became CEO. He had worked for us for eighteen years and was leading the largest division in our organization. I knew there was too much conflict, and he had to go, but I searched for a solution that respected his contributions and his well-being. I had multiple heart-to-heart conversations with him, and we ultimately worked out a deal where he would be able to purchase one of our convenience stores. Eight years later, he still reaches out to me. Earlier this year, he shared this:

> "What you did for us at that time seemed so small and so big. I know the road has many turns; yours and mine have always been true and honest. I can never repay you for giving us at least the opportunity to be where we needed to be. You are the best of all of us."

A culture that seeks to promote justness must also provide safety. All individuals must feel safe to express their opinion and voice their concerns without fear of threat, intimidation, or retaliation. A Sixth Level leader will not always agree with or be able to accommodate the wishes of every team member, but she will always listen with an open mind, and she will never punish a team member for voicing a valid concern.

Justness also requires a mechanism for addressing injustice. Thus, one move a leader can make to promote justness is to establish a clear and safe way for anyone in the organization to lodge a complaint or report an incident of injustice. Let's face it: the CEO cannot be the front office of the complaint department, and many employees might be afraid to bring a complaint directly to the chief executive, no matter how open and receptive you might be. Consider tasking an ombudsperson or specific officer with this role and be sure to communicate to the entire organization that this mechanism exists—as well as your commitment to respecting the privacy and safety of the mechanism.

Complex Systems Create Nonlinear Effects

You've probably heard the phrase "great leaders eat last," and that's a nice way to express that good leaders put the welfare of their employees before their own. The Sixth Level model is more complicated than that. Leaders must simultaneously nurture the health of the organization, the welfare of the individuals, and their own well-being.

Companies are complex systems. Within a complex system, the impact of change or activity on that system can be nonlinear, nonpredictable, and nonidentifiable.

Your life is a complex system. For instance, if you do something in the family circle, it's going to have a ripple effect on the business circle, sometimes in invisible ways. You don't always know what those effects will be, and you don't always know the origins of that ripple effect.

Business and organizational leaders must manage a complex system that includes three life cycles orbiting at the same time: the business's life cycle, the leader's life cycle, and the employees' life cycles. And one business may have many divisions. It may have many leaders and many employees. Sixth Level leaders approach this reality holistically. All three cycles are part of a single organism, yet every leader needs to pay attention to the individuals and to the whole.

Accomplishing that requires building robust connections between and throughout the organization. A Sixth Level leader must make sure that every member of the team feels connected to the whole—so connected that they feel responsible for the well-being of the organization, not just themselves. Eventually you are creating a culture of mutuality in which everyone is nurturing the organization, is helping, listening to, and supporting others, is ensuring the safety of those around them, and is excited about coming to work every day, experiencing intrinsic motivation.

How do you create this groundswell of positivity and productivity? An effective technique is the rally cry. Lisa Lochner shares her organization's rally cry in her essay, "Strengthening the Heart of Human Connection." A rally cry is a phrase that people use in organizations to motivate and get people excited about their common purpose. It's something everyone remembers that brings them back to the purpose of what they're doing and connects them as a team, just like sports teams do in a huddle when they chant their own personal phrase that unites them as a team and gets them going for a game. You can do the same for your team to motivate and unite them. One benefit of a rally cry is clarity. People lean in, whether on a sports team or a project team, when they are aligned. When everyone is clear on the problem they are working to solve, they can feel connected and can hold each other accountable to and responsible for the same standard.

Another great way to build mutuality is for you to start personally connecting with your entire organization in meaningful ways. That includes sharing personal stories that are in the service of the team, admitting when you've made a mistake, and trusting your team enough to delegate meaningful tasks and allow alternate approaches and solutions. One example, shared by a contributor, was during a one-on-one with a direct report:

> As the goals were being reviewed, we were also discussing the right behaviors to employ to help implement new efficiencies. The direct report expressed that she was feeling like she wasn't being heard, that she didn't have a voice, and that she was not coming across as she wanted. I shared with her a time in my life when I'd felt I was "on the ledge" and wanted to better understand how I was being perceived by others, so I'd found a coach. I told her about the benefits of a coach and that we would pay for it from our professional development budget. She was receptive, and we worked together to find the right person. Fast-forward three years, and she is still using the coach and recently said in her last one-on-one that before she'd been updating her résumé each week and thinking about leaving, and now she is excited to come to work each day and tackle the challenges ahead.

Sixth Level leaders are not afraid to be vulnerable. Part of vulnerability is looking at yourself and realizing that not everybody thinks the same way, processes information the same way, or makes decisions the same way you do. When you share your own limitations and blind spots, you remind everyone that it takes a team to win the game, not just a single player.

Mutuality also requires transparency. Share news about the company, tell your employees about new plans and initiatives and goals, and prepare them for changes by giving them advance notice and explaining why those changes are coming.

Being transparent and sharing information is so important because knowledge is power. Spreading that knowledge and ensuring that all team members know what the goals are, how the company is doing financially, and how their job contributes to the overall purpose allows individuals to become owners and understand the bigger picture. It builds confidence and reduces blind spots. This yields more participation in solving problems and individuals asking better questions.

In this way you build mutuality—not just linear connection but a complex and robust exchange—as you embrace transparency, vulnerability, and respect for others.

All these tactics and mindset shifts overlap in our Core Differentiators of The Sixth Level model. Respect for others, fair representation, an ethic of care, ingenious decision-making, vulnerability, and transparency all work together to create a culture of Self-in-Relation promoted and protected by The Sixth Level leader.

We have been told that these behaviors do not belong in the boardroom or the C-suite. But we know differently. They are essential to a higher level of leadership, even more critical today in a global high-tech economy with the many crises humanity is facing.

Sixth Level leaders have many challenges. The status quo is entrenched; the steps to this new paradigm require ingenuity and the ability to toggle. Progress often feels like two steps forward and one step back. If they seem overwhelming, start small. Choose one tactic—maybe it's changing the way you make a particular category of decisions in your company. Then tackle the challenge this way:

1. Choose an entrenched tactic.

2. Critique the current practice to understand the underlying issues.
3. Create a new approach with your team.
4. Implement the new approach.
5. Regularly audit the process and outcomes.

The Sixth Level is reached when the four Core Differentiators are activated together. When The Sixth Level is experienced collectively and when connection is prioritized, this leadership mindset achieves generative profitability and life-affirming principles.

While mutuality, ingenuity, and justness require dedication and patience, in the long term, The Sixth Level business is more sustainable. When everybody's working together in a healthy community with these qualities, you achieve improved growth by eliminating the friction of competing interests and by engaging the creativity and energy of every member of the team. People feel safe to contribute and support a culture of intrinsic motivation. The power of intrinsic motivation is a tide that lifts all boats, individually and for the company as a whole.

As leaders across the world embrace Sixth Level leadership, we will awaken the human spirit that is born in all of us. Sixth Level leadership prompts us to create positive change and to meet the need for belonging and self-expression. Imagine a world where creativity thrives, respect for others abounds, and an ethic of care guides our actions. A world in which we can navigate uncertainty, adapt to challenges, and cultivate a thriving system that benefits all stakeholders and contributes to a more sustainable and equitable future. That world becomes real when Self-in-Relation eliminates abusive power. That world is within our reach, and it relies on Sixth Level leadership. It relies on you.

Join the Movement

By Rachel Wallis Andreasson

I DREAM OF A world where all leaders are compassionate human beings who work in ingenious ways to make every voice heard and who make decisions in just ways that yield sustainable profitability. I dream of a world where society rewards sustainability and success is defined by well-being and inclusion as well as profits and growth.

Embracing Sixth Level leadership promises to make this dream a reality. A world in which . . .

- We shift our thinking toward sharing power. Poor power balance is the central barrier to achieving Sixth Level leadership and culture within an organization. In her book, *Lead Together: Stop Squirreling Away Power and Build a Better Team* (2023), Tania Luna defines power as the capacity to get things done. When we deliberately grow people's power (including authority, autonomy, information, influence, and skills) and distribute it broadly (so it is never concentrated in one person or small group) we increase our collective capacity to achieve amazing things. Imagine a world in which power truly raises everyone's boats, and no one is thrown overboard to sink or swim for themselves.

- Credit is given to the originator of an idea. So many times I hear women share examples of being in a board room or meeting and sharing an idea that is disregarded or dismissed. Later in that same meeting, a man shares the same idea, and it takes off. For example, Rosalind Elsie Franklin was a critical participant in the discovery of the structure of DNA but was rendered invisible while two male scientists, James Watson and Francis Crick, were awarded a Nobel Prize.[1] If credit were given to the originator, I wonder how much more intrinsic value there would be causing better ideas to surface.

- We honor the attributes that all individuals bring forth. I remember other leaders telling me I was "too emotional" or "too concerned about the people." I've heard many women accused of being too "motherly," as if that were an insult. On the flip side, when I've asserted my authority, I've been tagged as "too aggressive" or "bitchy." There have been many labels to downplay the important leadership attributes I bring to the table. We need to affirm women's competitive spirit and drive to win that typically dominates male leadership; honors all our best attributes, male and female, and in the domestic realm.

- We shift our thinking toward empowering all. Power is the central barrier to achieving Sixth Level leadership and culture within an organization. Tania Luna[2] introduces five power-sharing strategies that support Sixth Level leadership: authority, autonomy, information, influence, and skills. Imagine a world in which power means the tide truly raises everyone's boats, and no one is thrown overboard to sink or swim for themselves.

- Initiatives are funded to further equity in the workplace and in venture capital funding. Imagine innovation that addresses injustice, such as innovating products and processes that would resolve health care, pay, and capital inequities. For example, in Julia Boorstin's book, When Women Lead, she describes the barriers women face when competing for funding. These barriers are entrenched in paradigms. Imagine the explosion of productivity, creativity, profits, and sustainability we could unleash by funding more women-led companies.
- We each have an advocate. Several of the women who spoke at "That's What She Said"[3] have been part of Rung for Women, an organization that works to remove barriers and provide resources for a sustainable future for women. Rung (www.rungforwomen.org) is an advocacy organization for women. We are proud to share the proceeds of this book with Rung to support their effort. What if each person had an advocate in the workplace? What if every leader took a personal interest in finding out what inspires and what depletes their team members?

Our vision for a safer, more joyful, more productive, more inclusive, and more sustainable world is within our reach—if we choose to change. But change is not easy. Bucking the status quo can be frustrating and exhausting. Staying dedicated to the principles of mutuality, ingenuity, justness, and intrinsic motivation can be grueling when economic winds blow strong or competitors are snapping at your heels. Replacing leadership styles reminiscent of command and control with The Sixth Level paradigm requires both individual commitment and cultural and organizational momentum.

And remember: our goal is not to attack current leaders in the system but to challenge assumptions. We don't reject men as leaders. Men, women, black, white, yellow, young, old—all can be great leaders. We reject a system that defines leadership as individual power and excludes mutuality, justness, well-being, and inclusion from its definition of success. The Sixth Level offers a new definition of leadership and a new understanding of success.

In writing this book, we found countless examples of leaders using Sixth Level competencies that we shared throughout the two-year research and writing process. Those examples brought us energy and momentum. If these individual leaders can pursue The Sixth Level virtually on their own, like most pioneers, imagine how powerful this movement will be when we teach and inspire a generation of leaders to model The Sixth Level to improve organizations and repair the world.

As individual leaders change the culture within their own organizations, that culture will spread to more organizations and to more segments of our society. Business is an engine of growth in our society where new trends from business pollinate throughout the culture. As we plant ideas here and model this new approach to leadership, the movement will build in strength and size. The rest of our society takes its leadership cues from the business world. As Sixth Level leadership infiltrates the business world, we will see Sixth Level leadership in government, in civic circles, in education, in health care, and beyond.

It will take brave and visionary leaders to change the culture. When we shift to this new formulation, it may trigger difficult emotions among all stakeholders. Leaders may be scared of losing control, not appearing strong, and not being valued. The easy way out is to retreat to the power cave. If leaders encounter challenging emotions within their teams, they may choose to ignore and dismiss those emotions versus leaning into connection. We are humans. We are wired for connection. But when we feel insecure, not respected, or scared we might not be able to adapt, and when we fear losing our job or facing the unknown, we can damage the delicate network that connects all of us in joint purpose. Sometimes quitting or firing someone feels like the easy way out, but in most cases that is not the solution because we have not addressed the root of the problem. Sixth Level leadership involves the hard work of investing time to help individuals grow personally and professionally and to create a platform for success.

We have laid out the principles of The Sixth Level and explained the extraordinary benefits of incorporating mutuality, ingenuity, justness, and intrinsic motivation into your business or organization. We have profiled eighteen leaders who have championed the Core Differentiators of The Sixth Level in their business, and we have offered guidance on where to begin in your own organization. But my experience goes deeper and started long before this book was conceived.

My leadership journey began with my dad. He worked throughout high school when his father was killed tragically at work and supported his younger sister in attending college. He then started his own company after graduation, sold that first business, and enlisted in the 101st Airborne. After he served his country, Dad began a new business: one convenience store on Route 66. He grew that one location to many. His philosophy was to surround himself with people smarter than him and to give them the reins to make decisions. If they failed, he talked with them about how to do better. If they succeeded, he gave them credit. The convenience store industry was male-dominated, but Dad surrounded himself equally with women and men. His outlook shaped our company, and even though he passed away over twenty years ago, his thirty years of leadership catapulted our family business and were a true example of sustainable leadership. I did not know it at the time, but my dad exhibited many of the values and behaviors of Sixth Level leadership, and he inspired me to honor those values and to believe in myself.

Change doesn't happen overnight, and it doesn't result from just one person. Sustainable leadership requires more than just a new kind of leader; it requires a new kind of culture in which the daily actions of all stakeholders create and support an environment in which individuals feel included, connected, and willing to go above and beyond for their organization. We must guard against bystander syndrome and expecting others to take the initiative. No matter what level of leadership you currently hold, you must speak up when you see injustice; you must defend the principles of mutuality and inclusion. When one person steps forward, she shows others what's possible. When leaders model The Sixth Level behaviors, they create a culture within their organization in which all members are Sixth Level champions. As we launch this movement, you are not alone. Even in writing this book, we faced challenges and practiced Sixth Level principles together.

If we work to put The Sixth Level into practice, we foresee a jubilant year, a socioeconomic refresh that commits to a new beginning— wiping the slate clean of the old, limiting leadership paradigms and restarting with a commitment to The Sixth Level. We believe that this is possible. In fact, we believe it is already happening. The sooner you join the movement, the sooner it will be a reality.

ACKNOWLEDGMENTS

Our Contributors

We could not have done this without the trust of each of the contributors, who were vulnerable in their stories and took a leap of faith in being a part of this transformational book.

Editors Who Helped Us

- Anita Brooks, Business Coach and Founder of P4 Power Coaching
- Shirley Jump, JumpStart Creative Solutions
- Marji Ross, Marji Ross Consulting, LLC
- Kristen Hampshire, Writehand, LLC

Psychologists Who Helped Us

- Judith Jordan
- Maureen Walker
- Tomas Chamorro-Premuzic

Our Sponsors

- St. Louis Trust & Family Office
- Michael Staenberg, the Staenberg Group

Our Collective Network

Rachel Wallis Andreasson—I reflect on the unique place that laid the groundwork for this book, www.kbarlranch.com, owned by my brother and sister-in-law. Being off the grid in Montana gave me the idea to fill the ranch with a weekend of women. I engaged Stacy Feiner and Dina Readinger as our coaches, and Women Supporting Women was born. I am forever grateful to my strong network of women friends who have stood by my side through all the ups and downs. I am thankful to all my male friends who have listened to me and cheered me on. I cannot thank my family enough for supporting the endeavors I choose to pursue, and I am so proud of my adult children, Tyler, Megan, and Jacob, who have been by my side for it all, and my daughter-in-law, Andrea, who is a blessing.

Stacy Feiner—I would like to first acknowledge the trailblazers and pioneers who came before and paved the way for progress. I'd like to convey my unequivocal admiration for the brilliant business leaders who I've had the privilege of coaching for making your leadership personal and purposeful and for proving the promise of Sixth Level leadership that ultimately led me to this book. Deep gratitude to my wide network of collaborators, near and far, who share a vision with me of a better world and who encouraged me to press on. To Sona, Margarita, and Stacy—my true and powerful role models. To my parents and my two brothers and their families, who never doubted me. And to my husband, Peter, and our two adult children, Olivia and Zachary, who cheer me on and keep me going!

Jack Harris—I am grateful to my wife and dearest friend, Deborah, who continues to support me with her wisdom and care and has helped me be a better partner and father over our forty-seven years together. My children, Jared, Alexander, and Caitlin, are great gifts and have delighted me at every turn. My father-in-law, Euan Davis, modeled for me what it is to be a gentle man. My family has enriched my life and brought me great joy. Thanks to my dear friend, Jim Spates, whose brotherly love has embraced me throughout my personal and professional journeys. My gratitude to my colleague, Chip Capraro, who cocreated with me a men's studies curriculum. Finally, thanks to my inspiring students at Hobart and William Smith Colleges, where I have taught and hung my hat for fifty years.

Kathy Overbeke—There are many people who have helped me with this book and an abundance of people who have sustained and helped me develop the skills and stamina to coauthor this book. I wish to thank you all: To my daughters and grandson, who astonish me daily and are the source of my energy and hope. To my sons-in-law and their families, who have brought even more love and wisdom into my life. To my husband, whose constant companionship and love have allowed me to flourish. Thank you to my parents, who showed me the meaning of care, devotion, love, courage, strength, and purpose. And thank you to my sister-in-law, brother-in-law, and sister, who bring me happiness and comfort. Thank you, too, to my nephews, nieces, and dozens of inspiring cousins. You all bring me joy! My friends are invaluable. They are my daily sustenance. Without their laughter, understanding, perceptiveness, and support, I would truly be lost. My list of thanks would be incomplete without thanking my extraordinary coauthors, the exemplary women who contributed their narratives and the emerging leaders. Writing this book has been an unexpected and powerful journey, and I am deeply grateful to Dr. Stacy Feiner for inviting me into this project.

Our Publisher

We thank Amplify Publishing Group for patiently working with us and putting together such an awesome team to support us. Shout-out to: Josh Linkner, Board Chair; Naren Aryal, CEO and Publisher; Lauren Magnussen, Director of Production; Sky Wilson, Director of Marketing; and the rest of the Amplify team.

ENDNOTES

Chapter 1

1   Hazel Skelsey Guest (2014) has argued that Maslow matured his theory to include "metaneeds"—"the need to pursue intrinsic values that transcend self-interest, as a sixth distinct level beyond the need to self-actualise." Ironically, he failed to realize it, and it disappeared.

Chapter 2

1   "The pandemic had a near-immediate effect on women's employment. One in four women are considering leaving the workforce or downshifting their careers versus one in five men. While all women have been impacted, three major groups have experienced some of the largest challenges: working mothers, women in senior management positions, and Black women. This disparity came across as particularly stark with parents of kids under ten: the rate at which women in this group were considering leaving was ten percentage points higher than for men. And women in heterosexual dual-career couples who have children also reported larger increases in their time spent on household responsibilities since the pandemic began" (McKinsey & Company, 2021).

2   The mythology of gender dominant within cultural representations of males, reflecting normative behavioral ideals for males in a culture in a particular period, promoting stereotypical masculine heterosexual values. This dominant masculinity sustains the subordination of women and of men who represent marginalized masculinities (such as gay men). In contemporary Western cultures, masculinity is typically associated with personality traits such as independence and competitiveness, role behaviors such as being the primary provider and initiative-taking, and physical characteristics such as muscularity and a deep voice. However, the form of masculinity occupying the hegemonic position in a culture at any particular time is always contestable (Scott and Marshall, 2009).

3 Miller understands that women's psychology exists in a historical and sociological context. She does not provide the history or details of that context. We rely on Elise Boulding's work to fill in that history and sociology.

4 Indeed, mythologies about biological differences abound. See the recent 2023 publication in *PloS One*, "The Myth of Man the Hunter: Women's Contribution to the Hunt across Ethnographic Contexts." The authors report that "the sexual division of labor among human foraging populations has typically been recognized as involving males as hunters and females as gatherers. Recent archeological research has questioned this paradigm with evidence that females hunted (and went to war) throughout the *Homo sapiens* lineage . . ."

5 "These lessons extend beyond crisis situations and into the everyday modern workplace. Research has consistently found women tend to adopt a more transformational leadership style, which includes demonstrating compassion, care, concern, respect, and equality. In contrast, men have a more transactional approach, which includes a more task-focused, achievement-oriented and directive style of management." King, Michelle P. (2020). "Women are Better Leaders. The Pandemic Proves It." Retrieved from https://www.cnn.com/2020/05/05/perspectives/women-leaders-coronavirus/index.html

6 This is not to say that all social worlds are patriarchal. Boulding (1976) argues that women had power in several historical epochs, and there is evidence that the Iroquois Confederacy's long house system was essentially matriarchal. In addition, matriarchy (sometimes matrilocal, sometimes matrilineal, and sometimes both) has been identified as the structure of several ethnic tribal groups residing in Vietnam such as the Cham, Chu Ru, E de, Gia Rai, Mnong, and Raglai. Vietnam News Agency. (1996). *Vietnam: Image of the Community of 54 Ethnic Groups.* Hanoi: The Ethnic Cultures Publishing House.

7 These patterns exist in models of masculinity in many countries around the world, and structures of domination persist, despite significant cultural and historical differences. For example, similar distortions exist in countries as diverse as Vietnam, France, England, and Japan.

8 Defined by Kimberlé Krenshaw (1989) as "a prism for seeing the way in which various forms of inequality often operate together and exacerbate each other."

Chapter 3

1 Clymer, Adam. (2001). "Book Says Nixon Considered a Woman for Supreme Court." *The New York Times*. Retrieved from https://www.nytimes.com/2001/09/27/us/book-says-nixonconsidered-a-woman-for-supreme-court.html

2 Brescoll, Victoria L. (2016). "Leading with Their Hearts? How Gender Stereotypes of Emotion Lead to Biased Evaluations of Female Leaders." *The Leadership Quarterly 27*(3), 415-428. https://doi.org/10.1016/j.leaqua.2016.02.005

3 Benmira, Sihame, and Moyosolu Agboola. (2021). "Evolution of Leadership Theory." *BMJ Leader 5*. https://doi.org/10.1136/leader-2020-000296.

4 Benmira and Agboola, "Evolution of Leadership Theory."

5 Greenleaf Center for Servant Leadership. (n.d.). "What Is Servant Leadership?" Retrieved from https://www.greenleaf.org/what-is-servant-leadership/

6 Goleman, Daniel. (2014). *What Makes a Leader?: Why Emotional Intelligence Matters*. Boston: Harvard Business School Press.

7 Goleman, Daniel, Boyatzsis, Richard E., and McKee, Annie. (2002). *Primal Leadership: Realizing the Power of Emotional Intelligence*. Boston: Harvard Business School Press.

8 O'Reilly, Charles A. and Michael L. Tushman. (2004). "The Ambidextrous Organization," *Harvard Business Review*. Retrieved from https://hbr.org/2004/04/the-ambidextrous-organization

9 Surrey, Janet L. (1985). "Self-in-Relation: A Theory of Women's Development."

10 JBMTI. "JBMTI." (n.d.). Retrieved from: https://www.wcwonline.org/JBMTI-Site/history

11 Jordan, Judith V., et al. (1991). *Women's Growth in Connections: Writings from the Stone Center*. New York: The Guilford Press.

12 Goleman, Boyatzsis, Richard E., and McKee, Annie, *Primal Leadership*, 6.

13 Goleman, Boyatzsis, Richard E., and McKee, Annie, *Primal Leadership*, 21.

14 Goleman, Boyatzsis, Richard E., and McKee, Annie, *Primal Leadership*, 30.

15 Goleman, Boyatzsis, Richard E., and McKee, Annie, *Primal Leadership*, 39.

16 Goleman, Boyatzsis, Richard E., and McKee, Annie, *Primal Leadership*, 45-48.

17 Goleman, Boyatzsis, Richard E., and McKee, Annie, *Primal Leadership*, 51.

18 Goleman, Boyatzsis, Richard E., and McKee, Annie, *Primal Leadership*, 48.

19 Goleman, Boyatzsis, Richard E., and McKee, Annie, *Primal Leadership*, 48.

20 Goleman, Boyatzsis, Richard E., and McKee, Annie, *Primal Leadership*, n.p.

21 Goleman, Boyatzsis, Richard E., and McKee, Annie, *Primal Leadership*, 51.

22 Beck, Curtis D. (2014). "Antecedents of Servant Leadership: A Mixed Methods Study." *Journal of Leadership & Organizational Studies* 21(3), 299-314. https://doi.org/10.1177/1548051814529993

23 Jordan, Judith V., et al., *Women's Growth in Connection*, 13.

24 Jordan, Judith V., et al., *Women's Growth in Connection*, 14.

25 Jordan, Judith V., et al. (2004). *The Complexity of Connection: Writings from the Stone Center's Jean Baker Miller Training Institute*. New York: The Guilford Press.

26 Jordan, Judith V., et al., *The Complexity of Connection*, n.p.

27 Empathy. (n.d.). In *Oxford English Dictionary* online. Retrieved from https://www.oed.com/search/dictionary/?scope=Entries&q=empathy

28 Goleman, Boyatzsis, Richard E., and McKee, Annie, *Primal Leadership*, 5.

29 Goleman, Boyatzsis, Richard E., and McKee, Annie, *Primal Leadership*, 49-50.

30 Beck, "Antecedents of Servant Leadership," 301.

31 Jordan, Judith V., et al., *Women's Growth in Connection*, 55.

32 Jordan, Judith V., et al., *Women's Growth in Connection*, 55.

33 Jordan, Judith V., et al., *Women's Growth in Connection*, 57.

34 Jordan, Judith V., et al., *Women's Growth in Connection*, 46.

35 Jordan, Judith V., et al., *Women's Growth in Connection*, 21.

36 Jordan, Judith V., et al., *Women's Growth in Connection*, 29.

37 Jordan, Judith V., et al., *Women's Growth in Connection*, 29-31.

38 Jordan, Judith V., et al., *Women's Growth in Connection*, n.p.

39 Jordan, Judith V., et al., *Women's Growth in Connection*, 58.

40 Boyatzis, Richard E., Melvin L. Smith, and Ellen Van Oosten. (2019). *Helping People Change: Coaching with Compassion for Lifelong Learning and Growth*. Boston: Harvard Business Review Press.

41 Boyatzis, Melvin L. Smith, and Ellen Van Oosten, *Helping People Change*, 147.

42 Boyatzis, Melvin L. Smith, and Ellen Van Oosten, *Helping People Change*, 147.

43 Boyatzis, Melvin L. Smith, and Ellen Van Oosten, *Helping People Change*, 147-148.

44 Boyatzis, Melvin L. Smith, and Ellen Van Oosten, *Helping People Change*, 87; Boyatzis, Richard E., Kylie Rochford, and Anthony I. Jack. (2014). "Antagonistic Neural Networks Underlying Differentiated Leadership Roles." *Frontiers in Human Neuroscience*, 8, 12.

45 Boyatzis, Melvin L. Smith, and Ellen Van Oosten, *Helping People Change*, 83.

46 Boyatzis, Kylie Rochford, and Anthony I. Jack, "Antagonistic Neural Networks Underlying Differentiated Leadership Roles"; Boyatzis, Melvin L. Smith, and Ellen Van Oosten, *Helping People Change*; Friedman, Jared, Anthony Ian Jack, Kylie Rochford, and Richard Boyatzis. (2015). "Antagonistic Neural Networks Underlying Organizational Behavior." *Organizational Neuroscience*, 7, Emerald Group Publishing Limited, 83.

47 Boyatzis, Melvin L. Smith, and Ellen Van Oosten, *Helping People Change*, 85-86.

48 Boyatzis, Melvin L. Smith, and Ellen Van Oosten, *Helping People Change*, 9.

49 Boyatzis, Kylie Rochford, and Anthony I. Jack, "Antagonistic Neural Networks Underlying Differentiated Leadership Roles," 9, 12.

50 Boyatzis, Melvin L. Smith, and Ellen Van Oosten, *Helping People Change*, 86.

51 Boyatzis, Kylie Rochford, and Anthony I. Jack, "Antagonistic Neural Networks Underlying Differentiated Leadership Roles," 9, 12.

52 Boyatzis, Kylie Rochford, and Anthony I. Jack, "Antagonistic Neural Networks Underlying Differentiated Leadership Roles," 12.

53 Jordan, Judith V., et al., *Women's Growth in Connection*, 59.

54 Boyatzis, Kylie Rochford, and Anthony I. Jack, "Antagonistic Neural Networks Underlying Differentiated Leadership Roles," n.p.

55 Jordan, Judith V., et al., *Women's Growth in Connection*, 11.

56 Miller, Jean Baker. (1976). *Toward a Psychology of Women*. Boston: Beacon Press.

57 Jordan, Judith V., et al., *Women's Growth in Connection*, 11.

58 Jordan, Judith V., et al., *Women's Growth in Connection*, 12.

59 *Fortune*. (2023). "Women CEOs Run 10.4% of Fortune 500 Companies. A Quarter of the 52 Leaders Became CEO in the Last Year." Retrieved from https://fortune.com/2023/06/05/fortune-500-companies-2023-women-10-percent/

Chapter 5

1 Serrat, Olivier. (2017). "Managing by Walking Around." *Knowledge Solutions*. Singapore: Springer.

2 Boyatzis, Richard E., and Annie McKee. (2005). *Resonant Leadership: Renewing Yourself and Connecting with Others Through Mindfulness, Hope, and Compassion*. Boston: Harvard Business Review Press.

3 Rajgopal, T. (2010). "Mental Well-Being at the Workplace." *Indian Journal of Occupational and Environmental Medicine*, *14*(3), 63–65. https://doi.org/10.4103/0019-5278.75691

4   Held, Virginia. (2005). *The Ethics of Care: Personal, Political, and Global*. Oxford: Oxford University Press.

5   Vatanpour, H., Khorramnia, A., and Forutan, N. (2013). "Silo Effect: A Prominence Factor to Decrease Efficiency of Pharmaceutical Industry." *Iranian Journal of Pharmaceutical Research, 12,* 207–216.

6   Cilliers, Frans. (2012). "The Impact of Silo Mentality on Team Identity: An Organisational Case Study." *SA Journal of Industrial Psychology, 38*(2).

7   Dirks, Kurt T. and Donald L. Ferrin. (2001). "The Role of Trust in Organizational Settings." *Organization Science, 12,* 450-467.

8   Parry, Rosie. (2022). "Why Women View Trust Differently." Retrieved from https://www.london.edu/think/why-women-view-trust-differently

9   O'Brien, E. and Mary Rollefson. (1995). "Extracurricular Participation and Student Engagement. Education Policy Issues: Statistical Perspectives." Retrieved from https://nces.ed.gov/pubs95/web/95741.asp

10   Jordan, Judith V. (2017). "Relational -Cultural Theory: The Power of Connection to Transform Our Lives." *Journal of Humanistic Counseling, 56*(3), 228-243.

11   Prahalad, Deepa. (2011). "Why Trust Matters More Than Ever for Brands." *Harvard Business Review*. Retrieved from https://hbr.org/2011/12/why-trust-matters-more-than-ev

12   Talton, R.Y. (2010). *Dare to Restore Trust and Drive Loyalty in Distrust-Dominated Environments: A Stakeholders Perspective*. Ph. D. Dissertation, Case Western Reserve University.

13   LineZero. (2023). "The Positive Effects of Gender Diversity in the Workplace." Retrieved from https://www.linezero.com/blog/positive-effects-gender-diversity-in-the-workplace

14   Reiners, Bailey. (n.d.). "50 Diversity in the Workplace Statistics to Know." *Built In*. Retrieved from https://builtin.com/diversity-inclusion/diversity-in-the-workplace-statistics

15   SHRM. (n.d.). "Understanding and Developing Organizational Culture." Retrieved from https://www.shrm.org/resourcesandtools/tools-and-samples/toolkits/pages/understandinganddevelopingorganizationalculture.aspx

16   Hyken, Shep. (2021). "Leaders, Trust Is Your Most Important Asset" *Forbes*. Retrieved from https://www.forbes.com/sites/shephyken/2021/04/01/leaders-trust-is-yourmost-important-asset/?sh=893d4116fb22

17   McKinsey & Company. (2020). "Diversity Wins: How Inclusion Matters." Retrieved from https://www.mckinsey.com/featured-insights/diversity-and-inclusion/diversity-wins-how-inclusion-matters

18   Hogan Assessments. (n.d.). "Assessments." Retrieved from https://www.hoganassessments.com/assessments/

19   Inclusive Leadership Compass. (n.d.). "The 360 ILC." Retrieved from https://inclusiveleadershipcompass.com/the-360-ilc/

20   Center for Critical Success. (2017). "Why Trust Is Critical to Team Success." Retrieved from https://www.ccl.org/articles/research-reports/trust-critical-team-success/

21   Seppälä. Emma. (2014). "What Bosses Gain by Being Vulnerable." *Harvard Busines Review*. Retrieved from https://hbr.org/2014/12/what-bosses-gain-by-being-vulnerable

22   Zenger, J., & Folkman, J. (2009). *The Extraordinary Leader*. New York: McGraw-Hill.

23   Guo, Anna. (2022). "Why Team Connection Is Key To A Collaborative Work Culture." *Random Dots*. Retrieved from https://www.randomdots.co/team-connection-collaboration/

24   Flourish Leaders. (2020). "Cleveland Conference." Retrieved from https://www.flourishleaders.com/conferences/cleveland-oh/

25   Zak, Paul. (2017). "The Neuroscience of Trust." *Harvard Business Review*. Retrieved from https://hbr.org/2017/01/the-neuroscience-of-trust

Chapter 8

1   Blain, B., and Sharot, T. (2021). "Intrinsic Reward: Potential Cognitive and Neural Mechanisms." *Current Opinion in Behavioral Sciences*, *39*, 113–118.

2   Manzoor, F., Wei, L., & Asif, M. (2021). "Intrinsic Rewards and Employee's Performance with the Mediating Mechanism of Employee's Motivation." *Frontiers in Psychology*, *12*. doi:10.3389/fpsyg.2021.563070

3   Anders, George. (n.d.). Retrieved from https://www.linkedin.com/pulse/why-8-10-us-workers-want-employers-valuesmatch-theirs-george-anders/

Chapter 9

1   Boyatzis, Kylie Rochford, and Anthony I. Jack, "Antagonistic Neural Networks Underlying Differentiated Leadership Roles," n.p.

2   Gilligan, Carol. (1982). *In a Different Voice: Psychological Theory & Women's Development*. Cambridge: Harvard University Press.

Afterword

1   *PBS NewsHour*. (n.d.). Retrieved from https://www.pbs.org/newshour/science/meet-rosalind-franklin-a-sidelinedfigure-in-the-history-of-dna-science

2   Tania Luna. (n.d.). LinkedIn. Retrieved from www.linkedin.com/in/tanialuna

3   She Said Project. (n.d.). Retrieved from https://shesaidproject.com

BIBLIOGRAPHY

Arendt, Hannah. (1951). *The Origins of Totalitarianism*. New York: Harvest/HBJ Books.

Beck, Curtis D. (2014). "Antecedents of Servant Leadership: A Mixed Methods Study." *Journal of Leadership & Organizational Studies, 21*(3), 299-314. https://doi.org/10.1177/1548051814529993

Benmira, Sihame, and Moyosolu Agboola. (2021). "Evolution of Leadership Theory." *BMJ Leader, 5*. https://doi.org/10.1136/leader-2020-000296.

Bernard, Jessie. (1982). *The Future of Marriage*. New Haven: Yale University Press.

Bernard, Jessie. (1987). *The Female World from a Global Perspective*. Bloomington: Indiana University Press.

Boulding, Elise. (1976). *The Underside of History: A View of Women through Time*. Boulder: Westview Press.

Boulding, Elise. (1980). *Women: The Fifth World*. New York: Foreign Policy Association Headline Series.

Boyatzis, Richard E., Kylie Rochford, and Anthony I. Jack. (2014). "Antagonistic Neural Networks Underlying Differentiated Leadership Roles." *Frontiers in Human Neuroscience, 8.*

Boyatzis, Richard E., Melvin L. Smith, and Ellen Van Oosten. (2019). *Helping People Change: Coaching with Compassion for Lifelong Learning and Growth.* Boston: Harvard Business Review Press.

Brescoll, Victoria L. (2016). "Leading with Their Hearts? How Gender Stereotypes of Emotion Lead to Biased Evaluations of Female Leaders." *The Leadership Quarterly 27*(3), 415-428. https://doi.org/10.1016/j.leaqua.2016.02.005

Chu, Judy. (2014). *When Boys Become Boys: Development, Relationships, and Masculinity.* New York: New York University Press.

Chodorow, Nancy. (1999). *The Reproduction of Mothering: Psychoanalysis and the Sociology of Gender.* Oakland: University of California Press.

Clymer, Adam. (2001). "Book Says Nixon Considered a Woman for Supreme Court." *The New York Times.* Retrieved from https://www.nytimes.com/2001/09/27/us/book-says-nixon-considered-a-woman-for-supreme-court.html

Connell, R.W. (1995). *Masculinities.* Los Angeles: University of California Press.

Connors, R; Smith T & Hickman, C.R. (1998). *The Oz Principle.* Paramus: Prentice Hall.

Crider, Catherine. (2020). "Healthline: Stay-at-Home Dads: Statistics, Challenges, and Benefits." *Healthline*. Retrieved from https://www.healthline.com/health/parenting/stay-at-home-dad#challenges

Empathy. (n.d.). In *Oxford English Dictionary* online. Retrieved from https://www.oed.com/search/dictionary/?scope=Entries&q=empathy

Enloe, Cynthia. (1990). *Bananas, Beaches and Bases: Making Sense of International Politics*. Los Angeles: University of California Press.

Fausto-Sterling, Anne. (1992). *Myths of Gender: Biological Theories About Women And Men*. New York: Basic Books.

Feiner, Stacy. (2018). "All in a Day's Work: The Exceptional Practices of Women Leaders." Unpublished.

Fortune. (2023). "Women CEOs Run 10.4% of Fortune 500 Companies. A Quarter of the 52 Leaders Became CEO in the Last Year." Retrieved from https://fortune.com/2023/06/05/fortune-500-companies-2023-women-10-percent/

Friedan, Betty. (1963). *The Feminine Mystique*. New York: W.W. Norton.

Friedman, Jared, Anthony Ian Jack, Kylie Rochford, and Richard E. Boyatzis. (2015). "Antagonistic Neural Networks Underlying Organizational Behavior." In *Organizational Neuroscience*, 7, 115-141.

Gerson, Kathleen. (2011). *The Unfinished Revolution: Coming of Age in a New Era of Gender, Work, and Family*. Oxford: Oxford University Press.

Gilligan, Carol. (1982). *In a Different Voice: Psychological Theory & Women's Development*. Cambridge: Harvard University Press.

Gilligan, Carol and Snider, Naomi. (2018). *Why Does Patriarchy Persist?* Cambridge: Polity Press.

Goleman, Daniel. (2014). *What Makes a Leader?: Why Emotional Intelligence Matters*. Boston: Harvard Business School Press.

Goleman, Daniel, Boyatzsis, Richard E., and McKee, Annie. (2002). *Primal Leadership: Realizing the Power of Emotional Intelligence*. Boston: Harvard Business School Press.

Greenleaf Center for Servant Leadership. (n.d.). "What Is Servant Leadership?" Retrieved from https://www.greenleaf.org/what-is-servant-leadership/

Grose, Jennifer. (2023). "Dads Still Get Extra Leisure Time. Moms Are Still Subsidizing It." *The New York Times*. Retrieved from https://www.nytimes.com/2023/04/26/opinion/remote-work-moms-dads.html

Guest, Hazel Skelsey. (2014). "Maslow's Hierarchy of Needs – The Sixth Level." *The Psychologist*. Retreived from https://www.bps.org.uk/psychologist/maslows-hierarchy-needs-sixth-level

Hochschild, Arlie. (2003). *The Second Shift*. New York: Penguin Books.

Jayawardena, Kumari. (1986). *Feminism and Nationalism in the Third World*. London: Zed Books.

JBMTI. "JBMTI." (n.d.). Retrieved from: https://www.wcwonline. org/JBMTI-Site/history

Johnson, Allan. (1995). *The Gender Knot*. Philadelphia: Temple University Press.

Johnson, S. (1998). *Who Moved My Cheese?* New York: G.P. Putnam.

Jordan, Judith V., et al. (2004). *The Complexity of Connection: Writings from the Stone Center's Jean Baker Miller Training Institute*. New York: The Guilford Press.

Jordan, Judith V., et al. (1991). *Women's Growth in Connection: Writings from the Stone Center*. New York: The Guilford Press.

Kimmel, Michael, ed. (1995). *The Politics of Manhood: Profeminist Men Respond to the Mythopoetic Men's Movement (and the Mythopoetic Leaders Answer)*. Philadelphia: Temple University Press.

Kohlberg, Lawrence. (1958). *The Development of Modes of Thinking and Choices in Years 10 to 16*. Ph. D. Dissertation, University of Chicago.

Kouzes, James and Barry Z. Posner. (2023). *The Leadership Challenge: How to Make Extraordinary Things Happen in Organizations, Seventh edition.* New York: John Wiley & Sons Inc.

Laws, Judith Long. (1995). *The Second X: Sex Role and Social Role.* New York: Elsevier.

Levanon, Asaf, England, Paul & Allison, Paul. (2009). "Occupational Feminization and Pay: Assessing Causal Dynamics Using 1950-2000 U.S. Census Data." *Social Forces, 88*(2).

Luna, Tania. (2023). *Lead Together: Stop Squirreling Away Power and Build a Better Team.* New York: Skyhorse Publishing.

Lynch, John and Kilmartin, Christopher. (1999). *The Pain Behind the Mask: Overcoming Masculine Depression.* London: Routledge.

Maslow, A.H. (1968). *Toward a Psychology of Being.* Second edition. New York: Van Nostrand.

Mayer, G.G. & Mayer T. (1999). *Goldilocks on Management.* New York: Amacom (American Management Association).

McKinsey & Company. (2021). "Seven Charts That Show COVID-19's Impact on Women's Employment" Retrieved from https://www.mckinsey.com/featured-insights/diversity-and-inclusion/seven-charts-that-show-COVID-19s-impact-on-womens-employment

McKinsey & Company. (2022). "Women in the Workplace 2022." Retrieved from https://www.mckinsey.com/featured-insights/ diversity-and-inclusion/women-in-the-workplace

Mead, Margaret. (1935). *Sex and Temperament in Three Primitive Societies*. New York: William Morrow & Company.

Mernissi, Fatima. (1987). *Beyond the Veil, Revised Edition*. Bloomington: Indiana University Press.

Messner, Michael A. (1992). *Sport, Men, and the Gender Order: Critical Feminist Perspectives*. Champaign, IL: Human Kinetics Publishers.

Miller, Jean Baker. (1976). *Toward a Psychology of Women*. Boston: Beacon Press.

O'Reilly, Charles A. and Michael L. Tushman. (2004). "The Ambidextrous Organization." *Harvard Business Review*. Retrieved from https://hbr.org/2004/04/the-ambidextrous-organization

Piaget, Jean. (1932). *The Moral Judgment of the Child*. London: Kegan Paul, Trench, Trubner & Co.

Pleck, Joseph. (1981). *The Myth of Masculinity*. Cambridge: MIT Press.

Raworth, Kate. (2018). Doughnut Economics: Seven Ways to Think Like a 21st-Century Economist. White River Junction: Chelsea Green Publishing.

Rieff, Philip. (1975). *Fellow Teachers*. London: Faber.

Robb, Christina. (2006). *This Changes Everything: The Relational Revolution in Psychology*. New York: Farrar, Straus, and Giroux.

Serrat, Olivier. (2017). "Managing by Walking Around." *Knowledge Solutions*. Singapore: Springer.

Schur, Edwin M. (1984). *Labeling Women Deviant: Gender, Stigma, and Social Control*. New York: Random House.

Silverstein, Shel. (1964). *The Giving Tree*. New York: HarperCollins.

Sinek, Simon. (2017). *Leaders Eat Last: Why Some Teams Pull Together and Others Don't*. New York: Penguin Random House.

Spates, James L. (1976). "American Street Games: Some Sociological Observations." In *Street Games*, ed. Alan Milberg. New York: McGraw-Hill.

Wallace, D. F. (2005). *This Is Water: Some Thoughts, Delivered on a Significant Occasion, about Living a Compassionate Life [Transcript]*. Kenyon College.

Way, Niobe. (2013). *Deep Secrets: Boys' Friendships and the Crisis of Connection*. Cambridge: Harvard University Press.

APPENDICES

men and masculinity, the sociology of business and management, the sociology of community, and senior seminar research practicum. As a professional applied sociologist with specializations in gender, community development, and social organization, he consults nationwide for local governments about business process reengineering and project and change management. Dr. Harris has published on Vietnamese masculinity and gender relations, including coauthoring a book chapter in the *Routledge Handbook of Contemporary Vietnam* (2022) on "The Affairs of Men: Masculinity in Contemporary Vietnam," the article "Extramarital Relationships, Masculinity, and Gender Relations in Vietnam," *Southeast Review of Asian Studies, Volume 31* (2009), and "Incorporating Men into Vietnamese Gender Studies," *Vietnam Social Sciences* (1998). He has presented at numerous national and international conferences on gender relations. In addition, on the business side, he is coauthor of *The Municipal Computer Systems Handbook*. He has assisted in organizational analysis and design, leadership and management training and staff development, employee motivation, group dynamics and team building, conflict management and resolution, and the analysis of workplace culture.

 **Kathy K. Overbeke**, **DBA**, family business consultant, entrepreneur, researcher, and author, draws on her experience as an entrepreneur and practitioner-scholar to help individuals and businesses discover strengths to conceive new possibilities and reach desired outcomes. She is a family business advisor and executive coach who works with Fortune 500, middle-market, and small businesses. When working with family businesses, Dr. Overbeke aims to keep the entrepreneurial fire alive while maintaining family

harmony. She is informed by empirical research when helping family businesses plan for the future and when helping to develop leaders. Dr. Overbeke has published original research in academic journals and has presented her research internationally. She has also published in popular journals such as *Psychology Today*. She was an entrepreneur for over twenty-five years before returning to school to earn her doctorate in management. Subsequently she founded GPS: Generation Planning Strategies, LLC, joined the executive coaching staff at Case Western Reserve University, and became an adjunct professor of leadership, marketing, and independent studies at various colleges. www.generationplanningstrategies.com

Sam Allen is currently a doctoral student of organizational behavior at the University of Pittsburgh, where he studies how societal-level inequalities manifest within organizations. He is specifically interested in how organizational experiences differ along lines of social identity and how the authenticity of organizational messaging about equity shapes individual experiences.

Growing up in Lewisburg, Pennsylvania, Sam has long been interested in contributing to a society that affirms the equity of all and finds a way to achieve widespread prosperity to all groups of people. His interest in helping to address social inequalities led him to pursue a bachelor of arts in sociology at Hobart and William Smith Colleges, where he graduated summa cum laude while also minoring in environmental studies and public policy.

Dr. Jodi Berg, **MBA**, international speaker, consultant, and author, was the first female president and CEO of her family's fourth generation business. Wanting everyone to have the opportunity to live a purpose-driven life and create a meaningful legacy, she completely transformed the organization and culture, igniting unprecedented organic growth and catapulting Vitamix into an iconic brand and world leader in blending and high-performance cultures. Dr. Berg used her travels to over thirty countries to create a holistic, culturally inclusive approach to leadership, earning her praise for releasing individual drive and fostering team and organizational cultures that are authentic, transformative, and purpose-driven. Being identified as a national EY entrepreneur of the year was humbling, but her favorite recognition is being named as Owler's "Most Likeable CEO in Cleveland." Her personal purpose of helping people discover their wings and fly transcends every role she has ever held, from mom to business executive, board member, consultant, speaker, and author. Dr. Berg's published research on the impact of personal purpose on employee engagement, commitment, and life satisfaction served as the thesis for her doctorate in management from Case Western Reserve University.

www.frontiersin.org/articles/10.3389/fpsyg.2015.00443/full

Megan Eddings, entrepreneur, creative chemist, and keynote speaker says that entrepreneurship "found her" when she was met with a common household problem: stinky laundry. Tired of throwing away her husband's workout clothes because they smelled, Megan became obsessed with creating a better solution. With her background in chemistry and biochemistry from the University of Virginia, Megan invented a sustainable, antibacterial, and odor-resistant fabric, Prema. Since inventing Prema, Megan realized that she loves creating fabrics that protect the wearer and the environment. She always focuses on creating textiles that are backed by science, but she also focuses on an entirely ethical supply chain, meaning no sweatshops. Megan is a guest lecturer at the University of Houston, Rice University, and the University of Virginia. Megan is also on the University of Virginia's Houston alumni board. She even has a day, May 24, named after her by the mayor of Houston for her philanthropy work. Megan loves to relax with her husband, Kyle, and their rescue dog, Betty. She also loves to dance, laugh loudly, and laugh often.

Neeti Dewan, CPA, MBT, the Executive Yogi, is a world-renowned global finance and tax leader focused on international business growth strategies, M&As, and turnarounds. She has worked for over two decades inside some of the nation's top corporations like KPMG, Ryan, PricewaterhouseCoopers, Arthur Anderson, and Aramark Corporation. Ms. Dewan is a successful serial entrepreneur. She is the cofounder of two technology companies, HeyDiva (AI chatbots) and HeyDoc (AI health care), and an active investor in other technology firms. Known as the Executive Yogi, she is the author of highly acclaimed business books *From Executive to Yogi in Sixty Seconds* and *High-Level Leadership, Low-Level Stress*. Ms. Dewan has served on the Harvard University women's leadership board and currently serves on the Villanova University Institute for Women's Leadership advisory council and the board of the Indo-American Chamber of Commerce. She recently joined the board of directors of EV Hotel (www.evaihotels.com). Neeti achieved a master's in taxation from Villanova University and a BA in economics from California State University, Northridge. She's the recipient of numerous business awards and recognition for her leadership, including "Ten Best Women Leaders of 2020 and 2021," National Diversity Council's "Most Influential Women in Business" in Georgia and Pennsylvania, *Directors & Boards Magazine*'s "Directors to Watch," and "Most Successful Businesswoman to Watch 2021."

www.neetidewan.com

Jennifer J. Fondrevay, Day1 Ready founder and chief humanity officer, internationally recognized speaker, and author, is the founder and chief humanity officer of Day1 Ready, a consultancy that advises and guides CEOs, business owners, entrepreneurs, and their executives through the to-be-expected people challenges of mergers, acquisitions, and business transitions. As a successful C-suite executive who has led teams through three separate multibillion-dollar acquisitions, Jennifer turned her experience into a bestselling satirical business book, *NOW WHAT? A Survivor's Guide for Thriving Through Mergers & Acquisitions*. Her book not only draws on her experience but pulls from nearly three years of research and sixty-plus executive interviews, serving as both an M&A playbook for executives and a handbook for frontline leaders. Published in *Harvard Business Review*, *Fast Company*, *Forbes*, and *Thrive Global*, Jennifer is a frequent podcast guest and keynote speaker focusing on the power of embracing uncertainty.

Kirby Gilmore, MBA, is a native of south Florida and has always had an interest in entrepreneurship and business management. Prior to graduating high school with her associate's degree, she found herself creating multiple innovations, such as Site Staters (an online web design service), Kickback with Kirbz (an educational and entertaining YouTube channel), and K.I.R.B.Y. Co (an inspirational apparel e-commerce company). Her most recent endeavor has been creating and running a nonprofit, Kirby's Year Round Project, Inc, which provides donations and services to underserved children in her local community. Now holding an MBA in operations management and entrepreneurship, Kirby seeks to expand her professional experience in the ways of project management–related pathways.

Karen Grasso, professional employee benefit consultant and group insurance specialist, recently retired after a twenty-four-year career with a large national consulting firm. Karen was the business unit president for the St. Louis market of CBIZ Benefits and Insurance Services. She is multistate licensed in life, health, property, and casualty. As BUP, Karen was responsible for new business planning and development, financial forecasting, and growth and professional development of her staff. Karen served as an executive board chair of the CBIZ Women's Advantage board for over ten years. Her passion and contributions to the personal and professional growth of women both internally and externally have been recognized by many. Karen has been featured in both *Fortune* and *Entrepreneur* magazines and continues to support the success and provide guidance to both women and men in leadership as she navigates her retirement.

Sucheta Jain, life coach, cofounder and coowner, Farragut Systems, Inc, is an immigrant, entrepreneur, and business owner from New Delhi, India. She holds an MS in chemistry from the Indian Institute of Technology and an MS in computer science from Villanova University. In 1992 she cofounded Farragut Systems, Inc and served as their chief operating officer for over twenty years. Farragut was recognized by *Indus Business Journal* as one of the largest firms owned or managed by Indus women. Sucheta received the Impact 100 award from *Business Leader Magazine* and a Women in Business award from *The Business Journal*. Sucheta lives and works in Chapel Hill, North Carolina. She provides personal and professional life coaching services to help clients build their inner trust and establish lives and careers they love. A lifelong learner and lover of people, she is deeply inspired by her family, spirituality, connections, and interactions with nature.

Meghan Juday is chairman of the board, IDEAL Industries, and founder of the Lodis Forum. As chairman of the board of IDEAL Industries, Meghan has dedicated her career to working with IDEAL and other family businesses to help them thrive and survive. In 2020, she founded the Lodis Forum, an international peer group of female board chairs, vice-chairs, and lead directors to focus on governance excellence and peer exchange after recognizing the uniqueness of women serving senior board leadership roles. Meghan serves on IDEAL Industries and Kingsbury, Inc boards, the Brightstar Capital Partners advisory council, and several not-for-profit boards.

 **Ali Kindle Hogan** (she/her/hers), founder and board chair of Rung for Women, is the visionary behind Rung for Women, an organization that inspires all women to climb the economic opportunity ladder. Rung's goal is to empower women to go beyond surviving to thriving, creating a more robust middle class for women and their families. The granddaughter of the late Enterprise Holdings founder Jack Taylor, Ali applies the same spirit of entrepreneurship he exemplified, as well as the same civic commitment. After running the successful nonprofit resale store, Rung Boutique, for seven years, Ali was inspired by the women she met from organizations like Lydia's House and the St. Louis Internship Program to create space where women could get all of the resources they need in one place to achieve their vision for their career and for their life. In 2017, Ali and her team closed the store to focus on the next chapter of their story. Now located in the historic Fox Park neighborhood in St. Louis, Rung for Women welcomed its first cohort of members in March of 2021. At the new iteration of Rung, members gain access to coaching, career services, financial education, childcare, mental health services, and health and wellness opportunities, along with a community of likeminded women who are determined to succeed. Rung has brought together several organizations in one location in a collocated and coordinated model, including the Family Care Health Center, Provident Behavioral Health, Urban Harvest STL, and the Collective STL. Beyond her work for women, Ali is a longtime volunteer and board member for the Humane Society of St. Louis. She has assisted the organization in its development, animal rescue, public relations, and education efforts and is a member of the Friends Council. She also serves as a board member for the school attended by her two daughters, Kylie and Kenzie.

Lisa Lochner, MBA, health care executive leader, is passionate about supporting and encouraging the team she works with to produce the best results for the people they serve. She is very proud of the community where she lives and raised her family. She served on the local school board for nine years. She was named woman of the year for her community while earning her MBA at Webster University. She has served in various leadership positions, including establishing a foundation board and fundraising activities to invest back into building stronger community outreach services. Lisa was the first woman to become president for her hospital in sixty years. Lisa is a driven individual who works to be a servant leader to the community she serves, continually on a quest to strategically grow and enhance services to enlarge the footprint of health care services to the communities she serves.

Elaine Russell Reolfi, MBA, behavioral health CEO and engagement expert, is CEO of CommQuest behavioral health, a 350-person non-profit organization that delivers mental health, addiction recovery, and social support services across Ohio. She came to the role after a long career in the industrial world dedicated to engaging people and moving them to action, whether that be customers, employees, or external constituents. She most recently served as executive vice president of HR and corporate relations for a global steel company before deciding to dedicate her business experience to sustainability of the nonprofit infrastructure that keeps communities strong. As a first-generation American, Elaine grew up in her parents' garment-lettering store, learning the fundamental business lessons that served her well as she went on to be in the first generation of her family to go to college, a successful executive in global companies, and a community leader who has worked to help others realize their potential. She has earned degrees in journalism and business, is married to a college professor, and is the proud mother of three.

Anne Richards, MA, SPHR, SHRM-SCP, C-suite nonprofit leader, leads one of the largest nonprofit organizations in northeast Ohio as the president and CEO of Goodwill of Greater Cleveland and East Central Ohio. The $43 million organization served over 18,400 people in its twenty-eight different programs in 2022, including unemployed individuals, those with disabilities or other barriers to employment, parents who have lost custody of their children, and survivors of sexual assault. Anne also serves as an officer on the Goodwill international board of directors and has served on many nonprofit boards. Anne holds a bachelor's in criminal justice and a master's in human development and counseling. She is a sought-after community speaker on several topics including leadership, DEI, and ethics. Anne has three children who either have graduated or are currently attending Ohio State University.

Lorri Slesh, MBA, aPHR, executive human resources leader, is a strong and genuine communicator who drives strategic growth in complex organizations with energy and focus. Lorri attended the University of Michigan, where she earned a BA in education with a minor in psychology. After teaching and coaching at a private school, she attended Kent State University, where she earned a master's degree in athletic administration. From there, Lorri joined and worked in a variety of nonprofit, for-profit, and start-up organizations, creating transformational change. Lorri's diverse set of experiences allow her to hone in on a challenging situation and solve the right problem with the best solution. Lorri is valued for keeping her finger on the pulse of an organization and building collaborative teams that ensure strategic alignment. She uses the powers of language and common sense to lead and, as a result, builds teams that are motivated to match her intensity.

Stephanie Stuckey, JD, is CEO of Stuckey's Corporation, which has been known for generations as a highway oasis serving up pecan log rolls and kitschy souvenirs. Founded in 1937 by her grandfather, W.S. Stuckey, Sr., in Eastman, Georgia, Stuckey's grew into over 350 stores nationwide by its peak in the 1970s. The company was sold in 1964 and sadly declined for decades under a series of corporate owners. Fortunately, Stuckey's returned to the family in 1985 under the leadership of W.S. Bill Stuckey, Jr. and is now being continued by Bill's daughter, Stephanie. The company acquired a pecan shelling and candy plant in Wrens, Georgia, in January of 2021 and has been scaling production of the Stuckey's branded snacks and sweets—including the iconic pecan log roll—to be sold in almost five thousand retail stores nationwide. Stuckey's also operates a distribution center in Eastman, Georgia, a fundraising business, a corporate gift program, and an online store. Stephanie received both her undergraduate and law degrees from the University of Georgia. She has worked as a trial lawyer, was elected to seven terms as a state representative, ran an environmental law firm, served as director of sustainability for Atlanta, and taught as an adjunct professor at the University of Georgia School of Law. Stephanie purchased Stuckey's in November of 2019 and assumed the role of CEO. Stephanie's achievements include being named one of the most admired CEOs of 2022 by the *Atlanta Business Chronicle*, being listed as one of the one hundred most influential Georgians by *Georgia Trend Magazine*, and being a graduate of Leadership Atlanta. She serves on the corporate board for Bealls, a Florida-based retailer with more than 550 stores. The Stuckey's story has been featured recently in the *New York Times* Sunday business section, *The Today Show*, and the *Washington Post*. When she's not running Stuckey's, Stephanie enjoys traveling by car to explore the back roads of America and pulling over at every boiled peanut stand and the world's largest ball of twine.

Dr. Rachel-Yvonne Talton, leadership trust and corporate inclusion expert, is a distinguished founder, scholar, executive coach, author, and speaker who has gained international acclaim for her expertise in leadership trust, diversity, equity, inclusion, belonging, corporate leadership, and culture. Her coaching and training programs have empowered thousands of executives at some of the world's most prestigious brands to cultivate trust, foster cohesion, and promote inclusive cultures. Rachel's "GodJob" is to equip leaders with the tools and resources they need to achieve success as they define it. Her debut book, *Flourish: Have it All Without Losing Yourself*, is a testament to this commitment, and she is currently working on her second book, which explores belonging in the workplace. Rachel holds leadership roles on several corporate and nonprofit boards of directors and is a founding member of the BOW Collective. She is also an advisory board member of the Women Business Collaborative and has been recognized with numerous national awards, including being listed as one of the 2022 enterprising women of the year. An adjunct professor who has traveled to over seventy-six countries, Rachel values spending time with her beloved husband Jim and her friends and family. She also enjoys community service, writing, art, and music.

 **Meredith Weil**, chief operating officer and director, Third Federal Savings Association of Cleveland, has been at the forefront of regional banking leadership for two decades, currently as chief operating officer of Third Federal, a $16 billion mutual savings and loan corporation. She serves on the board of directors of both Third Federal and its holding company, TFS Financial Corporation. At Third Federal, Meredith focuses on creating value for the organization's customers, communities, associates, and shareholders. During her tenure, Third Federal's assets have grown by more than 40 percent through geographic expansion and product and delivery innovation. An advocate for a vibrant and diverse workforce, Meredith sets an example and a standard. She has fostered an exceptional culture with a focus on work-life balance and associate satisfaction, resulting in an organizational turnover rate less than half of the industry norm. In 2019, Great Places to Work and *Fortune* named Third Federal one of the best workplaces for women to work. A dedicated Clevelander, Meredith is an active trustee of both the renowned Cleveland Orchestra and Hawken School. Meredith is a proud mother of two and, as an empty nester, spends her free time exploring and experiencing the great outdoors with her husband and partner in life.

Sharon Weinstein, MS, CRNI-R, FACW, FAAN, CVP, CSP is a certified speaking professional, award-winning author, certified business coach, CEO, and health care strategy consultant. The "Stressbuster," Sharon is a global thought leader, health care influencer, and certified speaking professional who brings three decades of senior executive experience to the table. Today, she is a business acceleration and work-life integration coach leading a top consulting organization, an award-winning author of twenty-two books and over 160 peer-reviewed manuscripts, and a TEDxMontrealWomen presenter. She gives emerging leaders and career professionals the confidence to speak up, remain calm under pressure, communicate effectively, and negotiate wisely. Sharon's work has taken her across the country and around the globe, resulting in inclusive cultures of collaboration within the public, private, and government sectors. Known as the "Stressbuster," she guides professionals to manage stress and crises in their personal and professional lives. She facilitates awareness of emotional and physical burnout. Sharon understands human behavior, and she empowers professionals to rethink the use of time and talent. Known for elevating individual and corporate connections, conversations, and cultures, she is a master at seeing challenges, creating opportunities, and providing solutions through WOWTcomes. She's ridden a camel in Cairo, been a delegate to the Women's Conference in Beijing, designed the foreign patient department at the Kremlin Hospital in Moscow (yes, that Kremlin), and played with the penguins at Phillip Island Nature Parks in Australia.

TABLE OF SIXTH LEVEL LEADERSHIP SOLUTIONS

Core Differentiators:	Mutuality	Ingenuity
What leaders can do	Foster connections— be available for conversations and support	Create a work environment that is comfortable for employees
	Make it safe to criticize and make yourself available to hear employees' ideas and experiences	Share forward looking and strategic thinking with board members and staff
	Acknowledge others— take an interest in their lives	Create affinity groups and activities that support both teamwork and autonomy
	Understand which communications work most effectively with your employees	Build mutually invested teams interested in achieving the same results
	Always act in ways that promote employee financial, physical and mental well-being	Let employees define professional development opportunities
	Use measurement tools to assess the level of connection among your employees. This includes being racially and gender inclusive to produce higher engagement, better retention rates, greater profitability, improved ability to attract the best and brightest employees	Pay attention to employees bearing various emotional states and address them
Outcome:	Generative environment that raises the boat for all and creates a win-win culture	Foster a culture of curiosity and innovation

Justness	Intrinsic Motiviation
Shape policies to elevate employees and care for their well-being	Offer Town Hall or group meetings to give employees the opportunity to share, listen and implement improvements
Develop trusting relationships that indicate personal needs will be balanced with organizational needs	Develop a statement of purpose and values (known as a vision statement) based on input from management and other employees
Be non-judgmental when listening to ideas	Ask employees and listen as they explain how they connect with the mission and/or vision statement and live out these statements
Acknowledge and celebrate positive contributions	Engage employees to improve processes and practices
Empower others	Engage employees in the leader's passion for the organization
Show employees that the organization cares about managing stress	Engage with employees at all levels
Equitable and full representation	Inherently compelled to go above and beyond

METHODOLOGY

WE WANTED TO LEARN what women leaders had to say about leadership and if they practiced leadership in a distinctive way. In March 2022, two of the authors, Stacy Feiner and Rachel Wallis Andreasson, started with a small convenience sample of nearby women CEOs, owners, executives, and entrepreneurs. This was followed by a snowball sampling, leading to a total of sixteen cases. As our thinking evolved, we recognized this work as qualitative and primarily conceptual.

Our hypothesis, based on Self-in-Relation theory and on the work of Jean Baker Miller's *Toward a Psychology of Women*, was that women leaders would reveal leadership based on mutuality, ingenuity, and justness, which resulted in leaders and employees experiencing intrinsic reward in their work. We relied on existing research on patriarchal social systems and on women's social psychology to contextualize the case narratives.

Participants were initially given this prompt to tell their story:

> We are writing an anthology illustrating ten to twenty powerful women leaders who facilitated successful culture transformation using their unique personal experiences, sensibilities, and humanity to engender the emotional connection necessary for sustainable change and profitable growth of their respective companies.

We would love it if you could do two things:

Submit two to three names of women you know that are in leadership positions by March 10, 2022 that represent these diverse voices

and

Submit a sample chapter on your own story by March 31, 2022 to April 8, 2022. A chapter would be one thousand to two thousand in word count and can be a "story" or a "how-to guide" based on how you built a culture through community.

Kathy Overbeke and Jack Harris joined the project, and the four authors reviewed the initial narratives and recast the following more refined prompt to solicit another draft of the narratives:

Please recount a specific situation or context that illustrates your leadership approach to sustainable and profitable organization and change. Tell the story in the 1,500 to 2,000-word range.

1. Describe your leadership approach that emerged or evolved because conventional models were not adequate or sufficient.
    *   Bookend it: Start by homing in on the situation you were leading and the outcome you achieved.
    *   Describe your leadership principles and philosophy.
    *   In the middle tell what you did (practice) to achieve your desired outcome.
    *   Think about it this way: "My essay suggests . . . My story is about . . ."

2. Highlight and expound on what you did and how you did it to achieve the goal; use examples; what did you expect would be the reaction of your employees? How did the outcome evolve?
   - Draw a picture for the unique effort. If you use the word "collaborate" . . . explain your version of the word. What does "collaborate" mean? What does "collaboration" look like?
   - For example, if you say, "Make the newest team members feel welcome . . ." what meaning are you trying to convey?

3. Try to express the experience you wanted people to have as you engaged them on the change journey.
   - What was the internal experience you intended to create?
   - What emotional experience did you want others to have?
   - What were you feeling inside as you tried new things . . . doubt, angst, courage, confidence . . . ?

4. Provide details on how your leadership approach works.
   - What was the expected and actual outcome, and how do you know that you achieved it?
   - How did this improve the performance of the company organizationally and/or financially?

Overbeke, Harris, Feiner, and an independent reader assessed whether one or more themes could be identified in each case and if and how they revealed the Core Differentiators of mutuality, ingenuity, justness, and intrinsic motivation. Case narratives were then sorted and reported by the Core Differentiator most apparent in the narrative, although virtually all of the cases expressed all four Core

Differentiators. The participants were asked to review the assignment of a Core Differentiator to their case for confirmation.

Participants were invited to collaborate in writing the introductory chapter and to comment on the drafts of the book.`